The Making of Modern Missions

By

STACY R. WARBURTON

Professor of Christian Missions
in Berkeley Baptist Divinity School

NEW YORK   CHICAGO
Fleming H. Revell Company
LONDON AND EDINBURGH

.

New York: 158 Fifth Avenue
Chicago: 851 Cass Street
London: 21 Paternoster Square
Edinburgh: 99 George Street

CONTENTS

I. THE SIGNIFICANCE OF MISSIONARY HISTORY . . 9

II. THE MISSIONARY PIONEERS OF IRELAND . . . 53

III. THE MISSIONARY METHODS OF THE MIDDLE AGES 94

IV. THE DEVELOPMENT OF THE MISSIONARY IDEA IN
PROTESTANTISM 120

V. THE SOURCES OF MODERN MISSIONS 150

VI. THE AUTHORITY FOR CHRISTIAN MISSIONS . . 173

I

THE SIGNIFICANCE OF MISSIONARY HISTORY

HISTORY is not a very popular subject. " The dead past," " the living present," these are familiar expressions. They imply that what happened in days gone by belongs to the past, and has no relation to our own day. We are now living in a new time, so we are told, with conditions, problems and possibilities of its own, and our business is only with these. The past has gone; we live in the present.

But the past has not gone. It still lives in the present. The present has the conditions, problems, possibilities that it has, just because the past was such as it was. Missionary history has immense significance for the present, for us who live in these times, for the tasks we hope to solve. For it has made us what we are, it has fashioned the times in which we live, it has given us the tasks that are ours. We cannot understand Christian missions today unless we know the past. And if we are to interpret rightly the present situations and problems we must do so in the light of past conditions and problems and of our understanding of them. On the other hand, nothing that we read about in history belongs wholly to the past. The same movements continue today, or there are similar movements to be seen; problems solved then have risen from their graves to vex us again; methods used then are, it may be, still to be used; and the lives and work of great pioneers still influence us after many centuries.

Missionary history has a value for us in its attractiveness

and interest, quite apart from its sober lessons for our work. There are adventures that read like a novel, romances that carry us off into a world of love and loyalty, heroes of great deeds and leaders in great events, picturesque scenes of life in strange lands and ages, mighty movements that have changed the world, a panorama upon which you can look almost anywhere and catch a thrill that will stir you to the depths.

I

Both the significance and the interest of missionary history arise out of the fact that the past is a part of the present, the present a part of the past. When we talk of history we are not speaking simply of events. There is a difference between chronicles and history. The famous Irish Annals, such as the Annals of the Four Masters, or the Annals of Ulster, were chronicles simply. They give a date and an outstanding event of that year; another date and event; then another; and so on. That is not history. History presents the relation of events, the chain of cause and effect, the story of century-long movements that perhaps reveal themselves only occasionally in changing conditions and notable occurrences. It is this unbroken relation, this steady ongoing movement, that gives significance to history—to the history of the missionary expansion of Christianity as well as to general history.

So events and movements have causes back of them. Illustrations in missionary history are innumerable. The evangelizing of Ireland and the great missionary enterprise that followed were the result of the capture and slavery of Patrick. The Christianizing of most of Anglo-Saxon England by the Celtic monks from Scotland came about through Oswald's exile, his stay at Iona, and his winning of the kingdom after the death of his heathen brother. The meeting of

Zinzendorf and three Moravian companions with a West Indian Negro resulted in the wonderful Moravian missionary movement. The adventure of exploration opened Canada to the Jesuits, as later it led Livingstone to the heart of Africa. South America is Roman Catholic today because the early explorers were of that faith and took Roman Catholic missionaries with them. The past condition of Negroes in the United States provided the soil out of which have grown present problems and needs. The remarkable group of early Christian leaders in Japan is one cause of the outstanding Christian leadership and large influence of Christianity in that land. So we might pile up the illustrations of the historical causes back of familiar events.

To be sure, history is not quite as simple as this. In every situation that I have mentioned there were many other causes besides the single one given. In fact, there was a whole group of causes, some direct and some indirect, some immediate and some lying far back in time. It is impossible to unravel the complex and often tangled skein of influences and to know that we have them all. Many factors have made missionary history. Some of them we shall note later. The point to be emphasized is that there are these factors, these causes. Missionary history, like all history, is an intimate chain of cause and effect.

That means that the present is the source of the future. Just as the present has developed out of the past, so the future is to be what the present makes it. Take missionary policies, for example. Concentration of work, as opposed to diffusion, is a widely accepted policy. It has grown out of experience that dates back as far as the Danish mission in Tranquebar and Carey's work at Serampore. Education is a phase of missionary policy that has been emphasized since the days of Alexander Duff. The development of the Church of the land, under native leadership, is nothing new; it has been an objective since Patrick, and even since Paul, and in modern Protestant missions has increasingly been brought to the fore. These are policies that have come out of the past, they are the gift of the past to us. Will future missionary work, of American or British Christians, of Chinese or Africans, have these same policies or different ones? That depends upon what policies we are developing for the future. Our own plans are the basis on which those who follow us will build. The mission fields of today have been given to us by the conditions of the past. We are where we are, in most cases, because our fathers went there. And future fields of work are being determined by our choices and plans. Of this I have more to say later. The methods we use, too, were mostly given to us by our precedessors. Where those who follow us will work will be largely where we direct their steps, and how they work will be according to the tried methods we pass on to them. Like ourselves, they will make some original choices, but mostly we are determining these things for them.

Or take the native church. Just now the policies of the earlier missionaries are being criticized. That is itself an illustration of what I am speaking about, the development of the missionary enterprise of one age out of the missionary enterprise of preceding ages. It is perfectly clear to us that whatever difficulties or limitations we are meeting in the making of a worthy Church in the lands where we are at work are in considerable measure due to what earlier missionaries and native Christian leaders did; and it ought to be just as clear that the successes we are meeting are in like measure due to them and their wisdom. From this we can sense to some degree the responsibility we have in the building of the Church of the future. Of course the same reasoning applies to the Church at home. If our fathers had not been so wide in their Christian sympathies, so persistent in their loyal presentation of the missionary message, so statesmanlike in their organization of the Church for its world task, we would not have the rich heritage we enjoy in the present missionary outlook and endeavour of the Church. And conversely, if they had balanced their efforts better, had informed the children as well as they tried to inform the women, and had taken a longer look ahead in their policies of promotion, with more adequate attention to the education of Church and Sunday school and comparatively less stress upon the financial needs of just the current year, we would be far better off today. You can apply the same reasoning to our own relation to the future. Decidedly we are determining now what the Church of our children will be in its missionary knowledge, its missionary attitudes, its missionary activity. So too as to the missionary aim. Just now we are discussing that very seriously, and some seem quite at sea. We shall not be at sea if we look at it historically. History has something very definite to teach us as to the aim of missions. For what we are to aim at in our missionary endeavour now or in the future is pretty well indicated by the aim or aims that have been followed through the centuries-long effort to establish the kingdom of Christ in the world.

Look back or look forward, and you view a serious, thought-provoking situation. Look backwards, and you see the leaders of missionary enterprise entering their fields, making their policies, adopting their methods, laying foundations for indigenous Christianity, setting in motion forces that will develop into one or another kind or form of Christian life, forces that have given us the conditions we meet today, the problems, the successes, the failures. Look ahead, and you see the Church of the future in many lands, the peoples won or lost to Christ, the deep or the shallow understanding of Christ and His Gospel, the clearly grasped aim of missions, true to their founder, or an aim diverted into side issues and less important phases of human need. The present is the heir of the past in the succession of events that have made the story of missions and brought us to the place we occupy. And the present is the father of the future; what that future will be awaits our word and our act.

II

I have spoken of the significance of missionary history from the point of view of its promise for the future. Let us look more closely and see the factors that affect and determine the missionary enterprise. Elsewhere [1] I speak in detail of certain major movements that may be thought of as sources of modern missions. Exploration and colonization form one of these, making known new lands and new peoples, establishing centres for the expansion of life in the new world, broadening the outlook of the people at home, and stirring Christian leaders with zeal to adventure for Christ. Trade is another factor to be noted; we see it enlarging the acquaintance of Christians and others with non-Christian peoples, developing the middle class in England to be the bulwark of evangelical religion and of missionary interest, transforming the political leadership in important mission lands from Roman Catholic to Protestant, and providing facilities for wide-ranging missionary transportation and communication. A third factor is nationalism, sometimes furnishing protection for missionaries and sometimes presenting opposition and hindrance, arousing among Christians at home interest in the far-away peoples and their evangelization, stimulating the organization of missionary societies, and actually providing missionary service on the part of governments. Fourth is to be mentioned learning, freeing and broadening the attitude of thinkers and the content of

[1] See Chapter 5.

knowledge, widening popular acquaintance with the world, developing educated leaders among Christians, and ultimately making the universities and schools centres of missionary interest and effort. Still another major factor among the sources of modern missions is humanitarianism, atheistic in its leadership yet influential among Christians, stimulating an unselfish attitude, broadening Christian interest, and directing missions in aim and activity into every reach of human need. Finally there is the evangelical movement, the climax of these major factors, vitalizing all other factors, bringing to the fore progressively the true basis of Christian missions, providing stimulating examples of missionary enterprise, laying a foundation for modern Protestant missions in the evangelical churches of England, and finally giving birth to Carey and to modern missionary societies.

But there have been other factors besides these that have affected the past. One is racial migration. The most important movement in the western world since Christ was the fifth century migrations of the Germanic and other peoples. In almost every way that can be thought of, these migrations affected the life of Europe and the future of the world. From the point of view of Christian missionary expansion they were of superlative importance. They completed the disintegration and dismemberment of the Roman Empire and gave the Roman Church its imperial aim and world activity. They provided the occasion and the stimulus for the rise of the nations of western Europe, with all that that involved in the encouragement or discouragement of Christian missions, the variety of missionary message and activity, the establishment of a Protestant Europe and a base for Protestant missions. They gave direction to the development of Britain and Ireland, turning Christian Britain back to paganism and necessitating its evangelization anew, and by the isolating of Ireland from continental contacts, giving that land the opportunity to develop its own distinctive evangelical Christianity. They provided in Europe itself an extensive mission field at the very doors of the Christian Church, when the Moslem forces were closing Europe in and were shutting it off from outside mission fields. These are direct results of the fifth century migrations; indirect results can be followed in political, social, intellectual and economic developments. The Mongols in the twelfth and thirteenth centuries swept across Asia, almost wiping out the widespread Christianity, and opening the way for the firm establishment of Islam throughout that part of the continent formerly covered with Christian churches, the fixing of Buddhism and other faiths in the life of eastern and northern Asia, the settlement of Moslems in India with its resulting influence upon the Christian history of that land, and the retarding of the development of Russia and the weakening of Christianity in that and neighbouring countries. The coming of the Magyars at the end of the ninth century divided the Slavic peoples of Europe like a wedge, so that those of the south followed the Eastern Church while those of the north turned toward Rome. Quite as significant in more recent times has been the great movement of European peoples across the Atlantic to America and the smaller movements of other folk from other continents, giving to American Christianity distinctive qualities and setting before it the opportunity and problems of its home mission task.

The crusades were another leading factor in the missionary history of the past. They had some favorable effects. They stimulated loyalty to the Christian Church and at least to the externals of the Christian faith. They developed an interest on the part of European peoples in the lands beyond Europe and in the peoples of those lands. The contacts which they made with the Moslem culture introduced new elements into the culture and life of the west. In the minds of a few, as perhaps Raymund Lull, they gave birth to the thought of Christian missions to the Moslems. But there were unfavourable effects as well. They aroused a hatred of the Moor and the Jew. They gave to Moslems a radically erroneous conception of the nature and true spirit of Christianity and fixed in the followers of the Prophet an unbending attitude of fierce opposition to the Christian faith. They caused the Christian leaders of the west to think of relations with Moslems in terms of military antagonism instead of loving service, and thus helped to postpone to the long future any missionary endeavours for them, as well as to discourage Christian effort for other non-Christian peoples. By fostering military activity they continued or increased the state of disturbance and chaos in Europe, and prevented the growth of strong and aggressive Christianity. The crusades represented and embodied a great ideal; but while they introduced some elements favourable to the expansion of Christianity their net result was decidedly unfavourable, and we are still immensely handicapped by them in our approach to the peoples of Moslem faith.

The changes of rulers and governments have been another factor—and a very considerable one—affecting missionary history in the past. I have pointed out how Oswald's becoming king of Northumbria after the death of his older brother, who had renounced his Christian faith, opened the way for the spreading of the Gospel throughout most of England. The overthrow of the Tatar dynasty in China sounded the death-knell for the Franciscan missions in that land. Three centuries later the change in rulers from Kanghsi to his successor Yungcheng, the one favourable to the work of the Jesuits in China, the other opposed, brought persecution and weakness to the widespread Christian enterprise. In Japan the death of the military dictator Nobunaga turned the tide, which had been flowing with the missionaries, against them, and the persecutions of the Christians followed, with the closing of the country to foreigners and to Christianity. Such instances are numerous. The attitudes of governments have been among the most influential factors in missionary history. And there have been still other factors which might be described, internal as compared with these external ones, some social, some intellectual, some religious.

If we turn to consider the present missionary situation, from the Protestant viewpoint, we can discern certain factors and forces that are now operating. Outstanding is of course evangelical faith. Vital religious experience, now as in the past, is a *sine qua non* of missionary interest and success. The consecration of missionaries to their task, the faithfulness of the Christians of the land in the face of difficulties, discouragements and persecutions, the spirit of fellowship and love in the relations of native and foreign leaders, the power of the witness given in word and life by countless converts and missionaries, the bond uniting the nationals of almost every land under the sun in the missionary task, the gifts and prayers and loyal support by thousands of churches in the sending countries,—all these and other phases of the Christian mission of today hark back to the living experience of Christ and the personal relation to Him. What success there is in Christian missionary work is due to the faith and the faithfulness of those who accept Christ's missionary command as the authoritative word of a personal leader, living and divine, and who believe that the world-embracing enterprise in which He leads is worth while—worth money and time and life itself. The faith of evangelical Christians throughout the world is the dominant human factor in the missionary movement today. And this is only the continuation of a force, a movement, that has been in Protestant missions from their beginning. In other words, this factor of the past still continues its influence, and if we would appreciate its power and significance we must trace it through its development and results in past time as in our own day.

Another factor influential in the work of twentieth century missions and in the framing of their task is education. How largely educational work bulks in the work of the Church and the missions in the East, in Africa, and in Latin America is familiar to all who know that work.   Nearly 300,000 pupils in China alone were enrolled in Protestant schools of all grades when the statistics of the World Missionary Atlas of 1925 were gathered.   In India the number was nearly 650,000, in Africa over 900,000; in all lands outside of the United States, Canada and Europe the total was more than 2,400,000. Almost every type of school is represented.   And the investment in buildings, current expense and other items reaches into the millions. Evidently education is thought of as a principal factor in the work today. Of course it is Christian education, based on a Christian interpretation of life and controlled by an evangelistic purpose or hope. The rapidly growing insistence upon educated leadership is a concrete illustration of the place education has in the missionary plan and outlook. Educational plans in the churches of the home lands are another illustration of the same attitude.   But all of this is due to the emphasis on education in modern life everywhere. Increasingly through the nineteenth century and into the twentieth the people of Western lands and more recently those of the East have become eager for knowledge. Schools have rapidly increased, newspapers and periodicals and other educational means have multiplied, individual horizons have widened, and through educational growth we have come into a new world. All of this has affected missionary policies, the quality and attitude of churches native to mission lands, the intellectual point of view of Christian leaders native and foreign, the interpretation of the Scriptures and of the missionary objective, the attitude of the people to whom the message is presented, the point of view of the Christians in the sending countries, and a host of other phases and factors in the missionary situation. Yet education is not a new thing. The intellectual factor has already been mentioned as one of the major factors in the making of missions in the past. Clearly the influence of learning in the missionary situation today is only a projection of the past into our own time. The problems and questions that face us in relation to education are outstanding and critical, and call for the fullest knowledge and the clearest perspective that we can gain. How can we know thoroughly the many aspects and phases of the educational movement if we disregard the past out of which it has come? Here again the missionary history of the past has something to teach us of today.

Trade is a third factor of large importance in the present-day missionary movement. The business men in non-Christian lands are giving a message in regard to Christianity just as truly as are the missionaries. For Christianity is thought of as the religion of the West, and the words and life of every Westerner are quite naturally taken as an interpretation of that faith. So that the business man, the manufacturer, the trader, may greatly help or greatly hinder the presentation and acceptance of the Gospel. The Opium Wars grew out of trade relations; but the treaties that closed the wars contained a provision securing protection and privileges for missionaries and their converts, which while advantageous in that day has proved to be an embarrassment to Christians now. The insistence of business interests for protection by their home governments is quite as much of an embarrassment. On the other hand, trade is a favourable factor of considerable importance, providing transportation, communication, useful supplies and conveniences, as well as financial help and occasional friendly advisors. Among the people of mission lands the results of trade have been both helpful and detrimental. The outlook has been broadened and the economic condition of some has been improved, while on the other hand the development of organized industry and the growth of the factory system have brought grave problems. Trade is a most important factor in the present-day missionary enterprise, but if we would get a full understanding of its meaning and possibilities we must see it in its development, we must trace its history. For trade, as we have seen, has been one of the major factors influencing the missionary movement in the past. And just as it prepared the way for missions and at the same time was a hindrance, so now it is an aid and a detriment. For the highest success in Christian missions we must Christianize business and industry. And all this applies or will apply to the missions of the younger churches when these seriously undertake the foreign mission task that awaits them.

A fourth factor in the making of the missionary enterprise and the missionary situation today is government. This too is simply an extension from the past. Governments in other days have helped to make the colonies that have become bases for the missionary work; they have protected the missionaries or perchance have persecuted them; they have even established and conducted missions. All this was important in the development of the Christian enterprise. But the attitude of governments today is quite as important. The limitations and regulations of Mexico, Turkey, China, Persia, Portugal, France and Great Britain affecting education, church life or evangelism in those countries or their dependencies affect in the most intense degree, unfavourably or favourably, the progress of Christian life and work. The treatment of Eastern nations by occidental governments, or African peoples by European governments, has a most intimate and serious result in the attitude of the people toward the missionaries and their message. The preparation of members of the Christian community for leadership in national affairs may be almost as important a part of the work of a missionary as the organization of church life, and the Christianizing of the home governments may be as influential in the success of missions as the contribution of large funds and the sending of many missionaries. To interpret and evaluate government as a factor in Christian missions one needs to discover the bases of governmental attitudes in the past, and to see what those attitudes and their influence have been, and thus learn how to gain the advantages and solve the problems connected with this relationship. Here the past can teach us much.

Still another factor today is travel. This seems to belong exclusively to the present rather than to the past. Certainly it has come to have a large place in its influence upon missions and upon the attitudes of people in the sending lands. The tourist business carries occidentals to almost all the lands of the East and even from the Cape to Cairo; while an increasing stream of visitors from other countries flows into and across Western lands. Some travellers are neutral in their attitude toward Christianity, some are favourable, some are opposed. The life and influence of Western travellers greatly helps or sharply hinders the propagation of a true Christianity in the lands they visit. What visitors from the Orient see of occidentals sometimes influences them favourably toward Christianity, and sometimes, unfortunately, sets them definitely against it; and the point of view of the people of western lands regarding missionary work is affected in very considerable measure, even among Christians, by what is told them by oriental visitors. Travel began with the adventurers and buccaneers of the early days; it is of a different character today. Yet we have something to learn from reading the story of the past.

Thus we can understand fully the factors that enter into the making of missionary conditions and the missionary enterprise in the twentieth century only by viewing these factors historically, studying them in their beginnings in earlier centuries, tracing their development, and discovering their effect upon the expansion of Christianity and the results and influences that have issued from them. In nothing is the connection with the past more clearly to be seen than in the persistence of the dominating factors of past missionary history and their continuance in the missionary situation of today. We shall be wise if we let history speak to us.

III

The significance of missionary history is strikingly seen when we attempt to evaluate twentieth century missions in the light of the conditions and causes that led to their beginnings in earlier days. The location of mission fields and stations, the methods that are employed, the lines taken by Church development, and even the aims and objectives in the enterprise, are all the outgrowth of the past, and have been determined by situations and attitudes of days now gone. Take note of the places which are centres of Christianity in missionary lands, like the ports. Yokohama, Shanghai, Canton, Rangoon, Calcutta, Bombay, all these are well-developed bases of Christian expansion and centres of church life. It is clear that an important reason for their present state of development is that they were most readily accessible when Christian missionaries first sought entrance. Then their growing importance helped to stimulate the strengthening of the work there. So also of the capitals and other large cities. Meanwhile other centres and stations have been opened farther inland and away from the larger political and commercial cities, but as they have grown the older centres have continued their development also, until with their many-sided work, their growing administrative activities and their enlarging educational institutions they have by far the greatest proportion of the missionary force and require the bulk of the available money. View the missionary map of almost any non-Christian land, read the reports of societies and the letters of missionaries, and this becomes clear. And what applies to cities applies to sections and provinces. Missionary work is best developed in such areas as east China, eastern and southern Japan, the Ganges Valley, South Africa, southern Brazil. They were the parts most accessible, or the governments were most favourable, or religious and social conditions seemed most promising. The order of prominence of mission fields goes back largely to the conditions that led to the initiation of the work. Of course other factors have influenced their development, but fundamentally we are where we are and as we are principally because of conditions or reasons determining the entrance of Christianity in the first place.

It is interesting to note also the peoples among whom work is particularly emphasized, as compared with some among whom little is done. One thinks, for example, of the Karens of Burma, as compared with the Burmans who outnumber them nearly ten to one; the Laos of Siam as compared with the dominant Siamese; the Copts of Egypt as compared with the Moslems; the white peoples of South America as compared with the Indians; the animists as compared with followers of the organized religions; Hindus and Buddhists as compared with Moslems. In the case of almost every group among whom Christian effort is emphasized the missionaries were drawn to the group because they were more responsive; the work prospered among them, while little numerical success could be reported among the others. It was assumed that God was leading to the more responsive people, and others were more or less neglected in proportion to their lack of interest in the message. It would be a very interesting and profitable study to follow up in particular cases the circumstances and events that led to the comparative emphasis upon this or that race or religious group. In general the reasons will be found to be much as I have indicated.

We have our present fields, then, as to stations, areas and peoples, principally because in early days we largely followed the lines of least resistance. We could enter this field but not that, we had better response from this people than from that. So the work became set in the directions it has followed. There were some exceptions—but few. Doubtless the very human desire to make a good showing and the feeling that success was to be reckoned in terms of the numbers who could be brought to accept Christ personally, as well as the knowledge, perhaps, that the boards and churches at home would provide money and reinforcements largely in proportion to these reportable results, were strong elements in the situation.

The work, well established, developed under the same influences that had dominated its beginnings. Accessibility and responsiveness have been prime factors. Institutions like schools and colleges, hospitals or presses have developed, the work has expanded into numerous neighbouring areas, with outstations and corresponding institutional development, until a whole system of church and institutional life has grown up around the centre, or in the field or section.

All of this development has required money, an increasing amount of it. Meanwhile other fields have become accessible, and the claims of peoples whose response is not promising press upon us. But the need of conserving the results already obtained, and the evident importance of the place or field and its work, naturally lead to continued emphasis on these and effectively prevent any serious consideration of the possibility of scaling down money appropriations and other foreign resources designated to these leading centres. The result is that there is no money available for new fields, and no missionaries to be spared if there were money; nor has the missionary interest of the churches of the land been developed to provide in any serious way for the neglected fields.

In general this is how the work came to be where and how it is. Have conditions changed? Are there any new factors in the situation? Do the same reasons that led to the choice of present fields or the emphasis upon certain peoples or groups hold good today? Are there any new claims that could not be considered then that should now receive attention? It is a truism that we are living in a new age. But every age is a new one, with new conditions and situations. And we who are living in this age can see many things that are new and that justify our raising the question whether we should continue to follow in the footsteps of the past or should change some of the fields we are stressing.

For example, the native Church has in many fields not only come to self-consciousness but raised up worthy leaders. Is it possible to transfer in a large way to the native Church some of the old established work and thus release some of the foreign workers for new fields? Of course that is the ideal and objective of missions, and in some small way, here and there, the objective is being reached. But in an un-exampled degree the ability of the Church to care for its own work has in recent times been revealed, and leaders have arisen who have shown themselves capable of wise leadership. Is this new element a sufficiently strong one to balance the elements that have brought us to our present situation in these fields? It is dangerous to be too bold: but it is tragic to be too timid. One senses the possibility that we have come to a time of crisis—that perhaps we shall not have again just such an opportunity as the present one to make safely the broad advance into new fields and among new peoples that we have long hoped might become possible. It may be that the new leadership among nationals has been given to the Church by God to make this hope a reality.

New groups are accessible to a degree that constitutes a new situation. This applies to the Moslem peoples, for example. To be sure there are areas of the Moslem world that are still closed to Christian effort, like Afghanistan and central Arabia. And there are grave difficulties in other parts, as in Turkey, in northwest China among followers of the Prophet there, and in the little known lands of central Asia. But against these limitations we can set the transformation in attitude that has come about among Moslems in many countries, the broader world interest, the development of modern education, the disintegration of characteristic Moslem social customs by contact with European life, the new spirit of toleration towards Christians, and even the interest in the Christian teaching. These and other facts challenge us with the question whether we are not called to undertake in a large way missions to certain Moslem peoples, by the same sort of leading that determined the beginning and the strengthening of the work we now emphasize. And if that necessitates our adjusting our present policies and relationships, shall we not see a divine leading in this as we saw it in the things that led us long ago into our present fields and work?

There are new opportunities also in South America. We have scarcely sensed the changes in the situation in that great continent, though the Congresses at Montevideo and Havana have opened the view to us. Here, as in not a few other fields, missionary expansion must be a joint enterprise of those native to the land and of the leaders from abroad, with the direction increasingly native, though with proportion of emphasis differing according to conditions. The

important consideration is that among intellectuals and
common people, among the Indian population, among the
people of the interior, there are new opportunities that call
for serious consideration of the question whether readjustment of the missionary plans of many denominations may
not be called for to provide a response to the new conditions.
Certain other lands, presenting pioneer conditions, might be
thought of also, such as east central Asia and parts of Africa.
Some of the groups I have mentioned are quite as accessible
as those were among whom we began when our present fields
were determined, and the same considerations that led us
then may perhaps be factors now.

In line with what has just been said is a third circum-
stance with its accompanying question. Has the time come
to reach out from the centres into the rural districts? To
do this would require a readjustment and redistribution of
work and workers. For, as we have seen, the great bulk of
our work, whether led by foreigners or by native Christians,
centres in the principal cities. One can hardly doubt that
the pioneers were wise in entering the ports and other prominent cities first. And they will remain, as in all lands, the
most influential centres. But the rural districts are terribly
under-provided with Christian opportunities. Here on the
one hand is the vast bulk of the population in almost every
country, while on the other hand Christian work is solidly
and permanently established in the central cities. To be
sure, the cities and their environs are not by any means
fully Christianized; leaders of Church and mission have
problems and opportunities galore pressing upon them there.
But how long shall we wait? When will the cities be fully
Christianized? The large cities in Western lands are still a
great mission field. We cannot wait until the work in these
centres is completed before we turn to the fields beyond,
any more than we can rightly refuse to carry on foreign mis-

sion work until our home lands are fully Christian. The country population challenges us. We have come to see in a new way something of its importance. Do not the conditions lead us now, as in the initiation of the work, to weigh needs and opportunities, and to make such changes and adjustments as may be needed to meet the present situation?

One other phase of the question may be mentioned. There is a widespread doubt as to the authority of Christianity, the supremacy of its message, the right of Christian missions. It boldly asserts itself among those unfriendly to Christianity, not only in non-Christian lands but in so-called Christian lands as well. And it has made its way into the thinking of Christians also, weakening their loyalty to the missionary programme and all too frequently their Christian faith. The question suggests itself whether we perhaps need to offset this weakening of faith by a bold attack upon a new and difficult situation, challenging in its newness and difficulty. We have reached almost a stalemate in the missionary situation, as I have already pointed out. Funds and workers are apparently not available for new fields, the native church has not gained the missionary vision or impulse, the present work presses upon us with its unfulfilled opportunities and its needs. It may be that nothing else will shake us loose and release the resources which we clearly possess except a bold, faith-challenging adventure into one of the practically unoccupied fields. Such an adventure would drive the Church and its members back on the realities of their faith and make them face clearly the uniqueness, the authority, the power of the Christian Gospel, and it would make evident in a new and large way to Christians of the younger churches and to those not yet ready to accept Christianity the reality of the Christian faith and the sincerity and purpose of the followers of Christ.

From this third point of view, then, missionary history has

significance for present-day missions. It leads us to examine the considerations that have brought us to the present situation and to our present fields of emphasis, and to inquire whether those considerations still have equal value and whether any new considerations have entered the situation. This is a very practical application of history. We must give attention to the study of the past if we are to face adequately the possibilities and duties of the present.

IV

History has its significance also in regard to the methods to be employed. For example, how shall we meet the new conditions we are now facing? Consider the highly developed self-consciousness of the Church in many lands. As already pointed out, that holds large opportunities for progress. It presents also problems, for the leaders of both Church and mission. This self-consciousness is something new, and some have been led to feel that the attitude of missionaries toward the Church in the past has been repressive. As a matter of fact there has been little to repress. The national life in which the Church was growing up was not characterized by independence and aggressiveness, or the Church had not developed leaders, or the leaders had not adequately learned from the missionaries or from direct contact with Western Christianity the significance and task and possibilities of the Church. So that the missionary was compelled to take the position of oversight and direction that some today are pleased to call paternalism. But now the Church has come into its own, and is in many areas ready and able to take the place of leadership. What does that mean in the proper and helpful relation of Church and mission, of native leader and missionary? What does it mean, too, in the work of Christianizing the land? It would be a serious misunderstanding to suppose that the Church in almost any of the non-Christian lands is adequately fitted, in resources, in attitude, in appreciation of its task and responsibility, to carry forward its work unaided. By and large, the Church on the mission field is very limited in its missionary outlook. It has been taught by the missionaries in the past to think almost exclusively in terms of its local task —tremendously pressing, to be sure—and the development of the nationalistic spirit has not helped to broaden its view. How are we to meet this situation? Elements from the past enter into it, the weakness of the Church in earlier days, the disproportionate emphasis under the leadership of the missionaries, the lack of self-consciousness in national life, the absence of a stimulating contact either with distant untouched fields or with the missionary Church of the West. And elements new to the present are a part of the situation, the rapid rise of nationalistic feeling in the Church as well as out of it, the new complexity of need and relationship and opportunity, the new attitude of complacency toward those who have not been reached with the Gospel but who are supposed to be " living up to the light they have," the challenging threat of secularism to forestall the success of Christianity. How shall this situation be met? How shall the churches of East and West relate themselves to each other, in view of the relations of history? How can the resources of past experience and history become available for the new churches of today? These and other similar questions arise when we consider the bearing of the past upon the new conditions in the development of the Church.

There is a whole list of questions that have come up in relation to governments in our day that were never known in the past. For example, the limitations put upon missionary and Christian education, the influence of governmental attitudes and actions in foreign countries upon the attitude of those to be reached with Christianity or those already reached, the provisions of new treaties and other international commitments that bear upon Christianity and missionary expansion, and similar questions. History has important things to contribute in the solution of the problems that are suggested. Take the relation of education to government. What led missionaries into educational work in early days? We are carried back in this question to Comgall and Columba and Ansgar, not merely to Carey and Duff. What developments have there been since their time, and how did they come about? What were the results of education in earlier days, in different periods and in different lands? What relations have existed in the past between education and government? What new conditions have appeared, and what new aims may be considered? In all questions of government the experience and precedents of the past are most weighty and important.

How shall we meet the new development of secularism and eclecticism? That carries us immediately back into the past to discover what the attitude has been toward religion and toward specific religions, what the aim of Christian missions has been, what conditions similar to these of the present are to be found in history, what developments of earlier and more recent years have brought these movements to the fore. To deal with these new religious attitudes as though they had dropped upon us out of the heavens is to approach them blindly and to deal only with surface conditions and appearances, instead of getting below the surface into the fundamental causes and forces and contributing conditions. The fact that we are facing what is largely a new situation does not release us from debt to the past; it only makes a stronger demand upon us to ask history for its contribution to the solution.

In the matter of method we may ask also, how shall we use the new resources that are ours? The funds that we have are greatly increased above those available a few years ago; are we making wise use of the increase? To be sure it seems as if we had no more than in the past, if as much. But that only emphasizes the question whether we are wisely using what we have. It costs more to do missionary and other forms of Christian work now; does that mean that we are to put proportionately more money into what we are now doing, or does it call for a reappraisal of our present plans and policies and perhaps a readjustment of work? We may well stop to inquire of history how successes were won, what part money played, how money was used. What of the Irish missions, what of the Moravians, the Jesuits, the early nineteenth century work, the ingatherings on the Congo and among the outcastes of India? What were the methods and what the financial outlay in the training of leaders? What has been the contribution of the Church to general education as compared with that of the state, and what have been the results? And now what new situations have arisen, what new factors are to be considered, what new principles—or old ones—can be discovered as to the proper use of money in missionary work?

We have new cultural resources. Literature plays a large and increasing part in our life. Travel is becoming the most common thing. The radio brings us messages from across the seas. Art is applied to advertising. From airplanes we write upon the sky. What shall we do with these and many other new resources of culture and skill in the work of spreading the Gospel? Shall we use the same methods as in the past or adapt them to our new resources? This is peculiarly an inventive age, and history has nothing just like it from which we can learn. But perhaps the leaders of the days gone by were sometimes slow in using the means that offered. Call to mind the marvellous use of art on the part of the Irish of the early mediæval period, in decorated

Scriptures such as the Book of Kells and in the metal work in which they were so skilful. And remember the richly adorned churches of Wilfrid in Northumbria, and the art so widely used in Roman Catholic worship. A proper and valuable inquiry would be what the results of such use were, what gains, what losses, how far the experience of one period was put to use in periods that followed. The Passion Play makes an ineffaceable impression on those who witness it; can drama be used as a missionary instrument more widely and more effectively than it is now used? The stereopticon has long been useful on the mission field; can the movie be used as effectively? The radio uplifts us as well as amuses us, and many are won to a new life through it or are deepened in their knowledge of Christ or His Word; what possibilities are there in this for the spread of Christian truth in non-Christian lands? The past has its questions for us to consider when we face the riches of our present culture. How were the resources of the past used? How shall we use those of today?

So we might face the question, how shall we organize most effectively? What should be the organization of the Church of the land—a question certainly for the Christians of the land to decide for themselves, but by all means to decide in the light of the history of the Church in all lands. What of co-operation? What of church union? What relation should the mission and the mission work have to the Church in the home land? Every one of these questions looks not only forward into the future but back into the past. What has been the history of the Church in the lands to which its message has been carried? What was the policy of Patrick, of Aidan, of Boniface, of Schwartz, of Zinzendorf, of Carey and Judson and Duff and the leaders who have followed? And what light have their experiences to throw upon the questions facing the new churches today? What has been the experience of missionaries and mission churches in past days in the matter of co-operation, what determining conditions, what attitudes faced, what difficulties, what successes? Trace the relation through the centuries between the home church and the mission it has sent out—what has been that relation? what problems? what results in the work? A study of past experiences should have a wealth of suggestion for us as we face these vital questions in our own day. In all these questions of policy and method that we are meeting under new conditions missionary history can be our teacher, leading us around the mistakes of the pioneers and helping us to duplicate their successes.

V

The story of missionary history is brilliantly illuminated by the lives of the great missionary leaders. And these great personalities provide a significance in that history that makes the history indispensable for us in our day and life. First of all, there is the inspiration they give us to emulate their achievements and successes. Their evangelistic victories stir us with the wish that we could win many to the kingdom as they won them. One thinks of Paul and the companies of those whom he called into fellowship with Christ and the Church. One calls to mind the tireless journeys of Patrick as he travelled throughout Ireland preaching the Gospel, and his success in winning such numbers to the faith that Ireland became dominantly Christian. One remembers Aidan and Cedd and Chad and Eata and other Irish missionaries of northern and central England who gathered so many followers to evangelical Christianity that even through the darkest days and still to the present it has kept its evangelical life. In modern times one recalls the success of John Geddie in the New Hebrides, on whose memorial on Aneityum it is said, " When he came there was not a single Christian; when he left there was not a single heathen." The names of William C. Burns and J. Hudson Taylor come to us, flaming evangelists of China; of John E. Clough of South India, leader in the mighty ingathering of the outcastes; of Paul the Apostle of the Congo, of Kimura of Japan, of a host of other nationals from early days to our own time. And we are reminded anew that evangelism is the supreme work of the Church and of the missionary. Are we giving it chief place in our missionary plans? Does it have the emphasis in our personal life that it had in the lives of these inspiring personalities of the past?

Missionary history brings us also the inspiration of personal attractiveness. There have been some marvellously attractive men and women among the missionary leaders of the past. Raymund Lull must have been such a one. He was not perfect—who is? But can you read *The Book of the Lover and the Beloved* without feeling that it is a true reflection of the author? The devotion with which he set himself to years of spiritual development in preparation for his missionary task, and the spirit in which he faced the Moslem crowds on the shore of north Africa, testify to the attractiveness of this bold pioneer of the thirteenth century. Zinzendorf, founder of the Moravian missions, had the ability to attract others to himself. So had Fabricius, the "extremely amiable" co-labourer of Schwartz in South India. Dr. Hepburn, one of the remarkable group who began Protestant missions in Japan, seems to have been such a one. Professor Moore says of him, "Few missionaries ever gained in higher degree the esteem of all classes of people."[2] And of David Livingstone it was said by one who travelled widely among the Africans with whom he had lived, "Wherever the footsteps of Livingstone are crossed in Africa, the

[2] Moore, E. C., *The Spread of Christianity in the Modern World*, 152.

fragrance of his memory seems to remain." [3] No one can be a successful Christian worker, in this land or in any other, who cannot attract others to himself. He must first attract them to himself, that he may attract them to Christ. Not a few who have been missionaries to their own people could be added to the list I have given. We are stirred to emulation as we see these attractive figures of the past.

These men had great powers of leadership, and a study of their lives and the work they accomplished is a stimulus to us to fulfil a large leadership in whatever position we occupy. More especially it calls us to a reconsideration of the things that may be expected to be achieved through missionary leadership. Some of these outstanding missionary personalities were strong in organization. Columbanus of the Irish Church and Boniface of the Roman Church were great organizers, the one on the basis of monastic rule, the other on that of ecclesiastical authority. It was due to the one that Christianity became so deeply imbedded in the life of the people of eastern France and western Germany and Switzerland, to the other that Christian life became consolidated and the Roman Church became dominant. The superiors and generals of the great missionary orders, notably Loyola and others in the Society of Jesus, have been statesmen, though handicapped by their subservience to the Roman authority and tradition. John E. Clough in South India was a master in marshalling his outcaste preachers and teachers in digging the Buckingham Canal at the time of the great famine and in organizing the outcaste villages under their direction. Many another might be mentioned among missionary names, and now we are beginning to see such leaders among those who are the products of missions in the churches native to the land.

---

[3] Henry Drummond.

Others have rendered an inestimable service in developing the principles of missionary work and setting them clearly before us who follow them. Of course Paul was the great pioneer in this, and we are indebted to the suggestive studies of Julius Richter,[4] Roland Allen[5] and others for serious thought on his missionary principles. A study of the missionary policies worked out by Raymund Lull may still be valuable, not only in carrying the Gospel to the Moslems but in other directions as well. A modern illustration of conspicuous leadership in developing missionary principles is Carey with his emphasis upon training of native leaders, the place of social ministry, the importance of the vernacular Scriptures, the value of interdenominational fellowship, and the central place of evangelism. And another is Duff, pioneer in the use of Christian higher education in missions, originator of such modern plans as the missionary department in the theological seminary, the missionary lectureship, and the quarterly missionary review. When we stop to consider the work of such pioneers as these, we are deeply moved by the thought of our indebtedness to them for the principles so valuable to us, and are stirred to give ourselves to a new study of Christian principles in relation to the missionary enterprise of today, and to test ourselves in the light of the principles these leaders of the past worked out.

Above all, there is stimulus for us in the beauty and strength of their lives. Beyond and above what they did is what they were. James Gilmour of Mongolia had scarcely a convert to show for his twenty-one years of service in the tents of the Mongols, but we reckon him among the great missionaries for what he himself was. The literary contribution of Henry Martyn was of high value, but his short life has moulded hundreds of men and women. So of David

---

[4] *Die Briefe des Apostels Paulus als Missionarische Sendschreiben.*
[5] *Missionary Methods, St. Paul's or Ours?*

Brainerd. And so of scores of other leaders in the missionary enterprise, foreign and native, Francis of Assisi, Raymund Lull, unnamed Moravian missionaries, Samuel R. Brown of Japan, Neesima of the same land, Bishop Patteson of Melanesia, François Coillard of the Zambesi country, with Pandita Ramabai, Isabella Thoburn, and other devoted women. Whatever else a missionary must do in his crowded life, he cannot omit a continuous, life-long reading of the lives of the great personalities of missionary history, for the lessons he will learn, the suggestions he will gain, and the stimulus he will receive for his own successful achievement. And these personalities have a significant contribution to every one who is related in any way to the missionary enterprise, at home or abroad, in the mission or the native Church,—to all, indeed, who are striving for the best in their Christian lives and their life's accomplishment.

It is important to inquire what the qualities were that made these great. One notes first their adaptation to their special task. How significant that William Carey should have been the one to whom was committed the initiation, in a large and permanent way, of the modern missionary movement. His adventurous, pioneering spirit, stimulated by the stories of his uncle and his reading of Captain Cook's voyages, his training in humble employment and practical industry, his early studies in botany and his later attention to languages, his relation to the evangelical movement and his zealous work as an evangelist, his interest from early manhood in great humanitarian questions, his training in what Culross calls " the enthusiasm of patience," [6]—these were some of the qualities that adapted him to the particular task that was his. One notes the same providential adaptation in others, like Martyn, Livingstone, Chalmers, Verbeck.

_____

[6] *Life of William Carey*, 6.

Change some of these about and you can hardly think of them as succeeding—Chalmers and Martyn, for example, in each other's fields. Another missionary might make herself a ridiculous failure if she tried to act as Mary Slessor did. Alexander Mackay seems to us to have been just the man to hold the fort in Uganda when the success of Christianity was in the balance, and James Hannington the one who possessed the exact qualities needed to open the road to Uganda with his life. God makes no mistakes. And how evident has been His leading is clear from the story of the choice and designation of the great leaders, and many of lesser fame as well. In the light of the evident importance of this essential of success we may properly inquire whether we are using sufficient care in the selection and especially the designation of the missionaries we send forth. Increasingly the importance of such care will rest upon the churches of the nationals in the choice of their own leaders and their foreign associates.

You note, too, the pioneer spirit in these great leaders. That was another quality contributing to their success. They were ready to face the unknown, with confidence and courage and the ability to win through. Some were pioneers in the adventure into new lands. Livingstone's name occurs to us at once. The spirit of the pioneer is in those words of his, "Anywhere, provided it be forward." But there was a great band of pioneers before him, making their way into parts little known, or even discovering new lands for Christian effort. The unnamed heroes of the Nestorian missionary enterprise who fared across Asia and set the light burning in city after city from Siberia to the Indian Ocean and from Persia to the Pacific, the friars who sailed with the conquistadores to the Americas or followed them to blaze new trails in Paraguay and Guatemala and California, the Franciscan John of Monte Corvino in China, the

Jesuits Brebeuf and Marquette in Canada and Xavier and Ricci in the Far East, the humble Moravians in a score of lands from Labrador to West Africa, Egede in Greenland, Judson in Burma, Whitman in Oregon, Williams in the South Seas,—we might go on with a long list of mighty names. The world is larger because of their efforts, and the Church of God has found new areas of work through their ventures of faith. Who can measure our debt to them? The missionary enterprise of today is built upon their labours and adventures. We can see the work of the present in its true perspective only as we visualize these pioneers who opened to us the fields in which we work today.

Others were pioneers in forms and methods of Christian expansion. A brilliant story of missionary devotion was written into history on the pages that tell of Ireland and Rome and the East, the story of the use of monasticism as a missionary agency. Brendan and Columba and Columbanus and Martin and Boniface are great names, and there are many others worthy to be named with them as monastic missionary leaders. Lull taught the Christian world a new way of showing to the Moslem the meaning of Christianity; he did not get quite free from the hold the crusades had upon the minds of Christian leaders, but he showed emphatically that the way of Christ was love, and that success in winning the Moslems was possible only through love and by revealing a God of love. The Jesuits were pioneers in organization, planning missions on a world basis, the imperial idea expressed in statesmanlike organizing and distributing of forces. Saravia and especially von Weltz pioneered in the development of the missionary idea in Protestantism, showing that Christianity is missionary in its very nature. Carey was a pioneer in providing the Scriptures in the vernacular as an essential of missionary work, and in experimenting in the rich variety of missionary methods that we have mentioned. Others were pioneers in other lines, in method and conception and expression. If we are to understand the genius of missions we must take account of its pioneer spirit. It has been the pioneers who have carried the Church out to new endeavours and new victories everywhere and always. And what has been true in the past is still true. When we settle down to a following of the beaten path, then the day of Christianity's expansion is ended. When we are afraid to pioneer into new fields we have lost the characteristic spirit in Christianity. The men and women who inspire us in the story of Christian history were bold and fearless, always pressing forward with a divine discontent. With the emphasis today upon intensive development in missions we are in danger of losing the essential missionary spirit. Next to the deepening of its spiritual life, the greatest need of the Church in mission lands is a wide-ranging missionary interest and effort, and for this the missionaries and the leaders of the Church must be going back constantly to the pioneers for inspiration and instruction. We shall never cease to be indebted to these bold spirits of the past.

But if we would seek for the essential qualities in the success of these outstanding personalities of earlier missionary history we shall find them in the realm of Christian character. These men and women knew God. Their experience expressed itself in different ways, but the inescapable thing is that the dominant fact in their life was the presence and fellowship of God. There have been plenty of notable leaders in history who have had qualities adapting them admirably to their task; there have been explorers and adventurers with the pioneer spirit. But what the missionaries of whom we are thinking had was something more: they had peculiar qualities fitting them to their mission and they were inspired by a restless pioneer spirit, but above all they were men of God, men who lived in His continual presence, men who were led by Him and were supported always by the consciousness that they were at work for Him. Like Paul they might say, " To me to live is Christ;" " I can do all things through him that strengtheneth me."

They were men of faith. It is hard for us to carry ourselves back into the conditions in which they lived and worked, but the more we can appreciate those conditions the more we shall marvel at their faith. It seems to us often that great faith is needed today in the face of the situations met by Christianity throughout the world. But consider what these earlier missionary heralds confronted: nations one hundred per cent pagan or Hindu or Moslem; the Bible and Christian teachings wholly unknown to those to whom they went; languages unwritten, highways uncharted, precedents wholly lacking, meagre knowledge of disease and less of sanitation, the Church not informed, the missionaries themselves not trained, and anti-Christian forces at work in society comparable to those that tend to discourage us today. But they were not discouraged. They had faith. And what they had we in our day and our situation must have. It is well for us again and again to go back to these men of faith and try to catch their spirit, which is the spirit of Christ.

So we might speak of other Christian qualities. They had need of sympathy and friendliness and patience and perseverance. And in large measure they had these. Robinson says that " the secret of Livingstone's success, as that of every other great missionary, was his capacity for sympathy." [7] In one and another of the great personalities of missionary history we note these high qualities. Not that these were perfect men—far from it, but in so far as they

---

[7] Robinson, C. H., *History of Christian Missions*, 320.

approached perfection in moral character they were successful. That is the point: their supreme characteristic, so far as concerns the qualities that gave them their high place in missionary history, was Christian character. In nothing do we need more to learn from them for missionary success —Christian success—in our own day and work than in this. These were men of God: everything else was secondary.

So in its wealth of great personalities missionary history has a significance for present-day missions. There is a glow of inspiration, a mine of information, an unending course of instruction, a storehouse of wisdom, in their lives and achievements. Their contribution to missionary expansion was not ended with their lives. It still goes on in us as we are inspired by them and learn from them.

VI

Missionary history has a significance for us in what it can teach us as to aims and methods and personal qualities. These we have noted. It has spiritual lessons, also. Some of these lessons have appeared in our study of the personalities of the Christian movement in the past. But the spiritual phase of missions is the fundamental one, and we may well give special attention to it here. There are very many lessons from missionary history touching the spiritual side of our task. There is a lesson of faith. We have already seen something of that in the great leaders of past days, and have noted it as one of the qualities that led to their success. Not only in the missionaries themselves, however, has faith been noteworthy, but in the whole Church in its attitude toward the missionary movement. Put yourself back in earlier days and try to appreciate the immeasurable obstacles that the Church has faced in its missionary endeavour. Think of the size of the non-Christian world. The little band of disciples to whom Christ committed the task of winning the world confronted the pagan Roman Empire. That was an enterprise sufficient to challenge even the resources of faith that we might suppose those had gained who had been inspired by the personal presence of the Master. But their task was relatively not greater than that which the Church of the fifth and sixth centuries faced. Beyond the Roman Empire the Christians of the first century knew vaguely of lands and peoples, but these were not in their thought nor within their reach. The fifth century brought vividly to men's consciousness the great " barbarian " world of central and northern Europe. And already the Church of the East, as the Church of Syria and Persia called itself, had discovered the vast multitudes lying to the east and had started on its mighty missionary movement across Asia. Here was a task equal to that which had faced the Church at Pentecost, a task to test the faith of the Church. But how heroically the Church met the challenge! One is not more stirred by the faith of the missionary messengers themselves than by the faith of the home Church, the Church of Persia, the Church of Rome, the Church of Ireland, as they faced the impossible and made their plans for world conquest, prepared the missionaries, sent them forth into strategic places, and made the missionary enterprise their own, confident of success. The world to be won was immense, the resources were small, the opposing forces were powerful, precedents were lacking, and the future was unknown. But God was all-powerful, Christ was the leader, and the Church had faith.

Not less can be said of the Church's faith in other periods, when the world had grown still larger, as in Carey's day and the days that followed. But faith was needed not only in the initiation of the enterprise, when the Church and its representatives might set themselves with enthusiasm to the undertaking of an immense task, but in the humdrum days of slow development and meagre results. There have been times of terrible persecution, like those of the Roman emperors of the first and second centuries, or that of the Japanese of the early seventeenth century, or those of the Armenians of the nineteenth century and our own. There have been days of slow progress, like the first half-century of Protestant Christianity in China, or the early years of work in Burma. There have been fields that have sent home meagre reports of ingatherings and baptisms, and there have been peoples and classes and castes among whom the Gospel has won no outstanding triumphs. But the Church has kept on. It has faltered sometimes, but its faith in God and the future has held it to its great missionary task. Faith has been the steady, compelling force that through discouraging conditions has yet kept the Church and its great spirits from discouragement of heart and made it certain of success.

The history of missionary enterprise has this lesson to teach us in our missionary efforts today—the lesson of faith. And as we follow the story through the years and the centuries and discover how the faith of the pioneers was rewarded, how the kingdom has grown and Christianity has expanded, we can see the power of faith and sense the necessity of it. Certainly we need faith today, faced with new conditions, confronting an untrodden way through difficult and dangerous situations, and meeting the insidious influence of secularism and doubt within Christianity itself. But a study of past history will strengthen our faith. History has no greater lesson for us than this. And we can mightily profit from the faith of the past in our mission today.

Another spiritual lesson from missionary history is the persistence of spiritual forces. I am thinking of some of the great Christian movements that for a time were highly successful and promised greatly, but were overcome by other forces and were wiped out by heathenism or were absorbed by a non-evangelical faith. One remembers the Nestorian missions, already mentioned.[8] They carried Christianity over most of Asia. Cosmas, the early traveller, found Christians in 525 A. D. in Ceylon, the Ganges Valley, Pegu, Cochin China, Tonking and Siam. By the eighth century there were Christians and a metropolitan among the Turks. In the eleventh century the Keraits, an important people northwest of China, are found to be Christian. In the thirteenth century Christianity was widespread in Turkestan and there was an archbishop at Merv. The inscriptions in the Christian cemetery at Semirechensk, near Lake Balkash in central Asia, tell of Christians from places and peoples so many and so widespread that Professor Chevolson, of Leningrad, thinks there were millions of disciples in central Asia. They were an eminent factor in the life of China through many centuries. They were in Tibet and Siberia, in Mongolia, and it may be in Japan. Twenty-seven metropolitans are mentioned, in Samarkand and Kashgar and Herat and other centres now without a single Christian. The light of the Gospel shone in hundreds of places from Persia to the Pacific and from Siberia to the Indian Ocean.[9] Then came Tamerlane and other terror-bringing leaders, and wiped Christianity off the map of central Asia, while in China and Japan compromise with non-Christian faiths, the opposition of governments, Roman Catholics and Moslems, and the separation from a base of spiritual support at home, did their work of destruction, and Christianity disappeared from view. Yet the spiritual force lived on. One may not dogmatize when proof is wanting, but missionaries are confident that the wonderful traditions of the Karens and other hill people of Burma, about a flood, and a book that told of God and was lost, and white mes-

---

[8] See also Chapter 6.
[9] Stewart, *Nestorian Missionary Enterprise,* passim.

sengers from the West who would some day bring back the lost book, find their source in the Christianity that centuries ago was so strong in southeastern Asia, and are a leftover from that great movement. If this is true, the spiritual force that expressed itself in the widespread Christian life of the early centuries has not been lost, but has again revealed itself in the marvellous turning of the Karens, the Lahus and other peoples to Christianity. There are those, too, who find in the Nestorian Christianity of China the source of Shin Buddhism in Japan, with its parallels to Christian teaching. Of this there is less certainty; we only know that its founder brought his ideas from China, where he had opportunities to meet Christian leaders and to learn their faith. We may yet discover in the little known regions of central Asia further living proofs of the persistence of the Christianity of the great missionary period.

A different case was that of the Irish Church and its missionary enterprise.[10] Growing up in the fifth and sixth centuries, when contact with Europe was infrequent and influence from outside was little felt, it held in large measure to the faith and practices of early centuries. It emphasized simplicity of organization and worship when the Roman Church was developing an elaborate ecclesiasticism and formalism. When sacerdotalism was coming to the front in the message of Roman missionaries it largely avoided this and held loyally and insistently to the Scriptures and their use. Great Irish leaders arose who established in many parts of their land monasteries as schools of Christian training, from which Christianity was carried into almost every corner of Ireland, and which drew students of the Bible from over the seas. Evangelistic zeal early developed into a wide-ranging missionary enthusiasm, and a stream of mis-

---

[10] See Chapter 2.

sionaries spread from the centres in the West across Scotland and northern England and western Europe, winning innumerable converts to the new faith. But the Irish missionary movement met the powerful Roman movement, and after a strenuous struggle Rome won and the Irish movement disappeared. I discuss elsewhere the causes; here we only mention the fact. But was that the end? I think not. To begin with, we have the fact that many of the centres of Christian influence established by the Irish monks continued under the Romans and lasted on as bases of powerful Christian effort. The Roman leaders added to what the Irish had done, but the success of Roman effort later may be traced back in large measure to the spirit and attitude of early days and the impetus given the work by the Celtic workers. Moreover, one wonders whether a permanent influence was not left in England, in the spirit of the people and of their religion. It may be that the eagerness for freedom and the independent attitude toward government and toward religion that seem to have characterized the English people had its origin in the teaching and influence of the free and independent Celts. It may be, too, that the evangelical spirit of the early Irish years impressed itself permanently upon the English Church, and that though hidden through many centuries of outside ecclesiastical domination it came to light again in Reformation days and became one of the influences that have set England on high in Christian service to the world. One can only surmise. Here is a fascinating subject for historical study. Perhaps we may discover that just as in Japan the Christianity established by Xavier and Fernandez and their followers persisted through the centuries of seclusion when the Christian faith was under the ban and was found still living when Christian missionaries once more arrived, so the evangelical faith of the Irish Church and its evangelists lived on, under other forms or in the dark, to issue in a larger and finer Christianity than if it had not been.

So again it may help us in our understanding of the present, our attitudes toward present-day Christian life and missionary principles, and our thought of the future, to look back into the past and to study the missionary movement of earlier days. Energy can be transformed but cannot be lost. What we do today may seem to lose its effectiveness tomorrow, but the day after tomorrow it will emerge in different form to continue its blessing to the world.

A third spiritual lesson that we do well to learn from missionary history is the greatness of truth. How many divisions and groups there have been among the Christian forces! Yet each has represented some separate phase of Christian truth, and all have contributed to the spread of Christian faith throughout the world. In that great missionary age from the fifth to the tenth centuries, there were four principal missionary streams that spread across Europe and Asia: the Irish, the Roman, the Eastern and the Nestorian. Each represented a distinct ecclesiastical idea. They had little to do with one another. Each thought the others unorthodox, with a message incomplete or imperfect. But God used them all. Every one was inspired by the same missionary zeal, every one made its contribution to the expansion of Christianity. The story of missionary history is incomplete without them all. So it was in later times. Denominational division has carried Christian missions forth under many different organizations, but each is making its contribution to the one common work. The glory of Protestantism is its variety of expression. And the many groups have each given their service in the one cause.

Organization is of course closely related to credal interpretation. In missionary history emphasis has sometimes been laid upon the one and sometimes upon the other. The

Roman Church denounced the Nestorians as unorthodox, and the Nestorians would have nothing to do with Rome. But each had the imperial idea, and each gave its best in the missionary expansion of Christianity. Roman Catholic Jesuits and other pioneers of that Church gave an example for all time of self-sacrificing Christian devotion, and Protestants have built upon their foundation. Among Protestants and in the Christian world in general there have been many interpretations of the common faith, but each has taken a place in the common missionary service and task. This is by no means to say that what is believed is unimportant: it is vitally important. The tragedy of missionary history is the devotion of some of the notable missionaries to the carrying of a message that was based upon a false interpretation of Christian truth. But the fact that God seems to have used them all emphasizes the greatness of that truth. It may mean also that in spite of the things we have perhaps emphasized more, the common fundamentals are the powerful forces that have achieved the true and lasting results.

The greatness of Christian truth is seen also in the varied methods in which missionaries have expressed the message. Some have been evangelists, like the members of the China Inland Mission, and have given little place to other forms of work. Some have devoted themselves to social ministry, as did many of the monastic groups of mediæval days, in the attempt to build a Christian society. Some have given their effort to education, like the teaching orders of the Roman missions and the great company of Protestant teachers in modern missions, to capture the mind for Christ and to develop an intelligent Christian community with trained leaders. The debate as to the validity of various methods is not a new one. Many methods have been used and the message has been given in many forms. And many others will yet appear. A study of the past should make us realize the wealth of variety that is possible in presenting our message, and the broad reach of truth as it is expressed in Christian activity. If we read history with open mind, we shall learn a lesson of vast importance as to the greatness of the truth of Christ. In these days of emphasis upon consolidation and union and standardization we shall see the place that variety of organization has had in the spread of the faith. In a day of doubt as to the Christian message on the one hand, and of syncretism on the other, we shall appreciate the importance of evaluating interpretations of Christianity and of discovering the true interpretation. In the midst of a bewildering diversity of form and method we shall see the value of all and try to find the just place and the most effective use of each. And above all we shall realize that truth is larger than all we have yet learned, and that we must still study and learn and press on to the full knowledge of God's truth, that we may make known that truth in all its fulness to mankind.

II

THE MISSIONARY PIONEERS OF IRELAND

FOUR streams of Christian missions have been mentioned that flowed across Asia and Europe in the early Middle Ages. One went out from the Church of the East, or the Nestorian Church, and spread over most of Asia in the marvellous way described elsewhere.[1] The three others were in Europe. One represented the churches of the eastern empire and flowed northward from Constantinople through the Slavic lands of eastern Europe; a second took its rise in Ireland and carried the Gospel into Scotland and England and across western Europe; the third was the Roman missionary enterprise, which ultimately absorbed in large part the two other European streams. Many of us are more or less familiar with the streams that flowed from Constantinople and Rome, especially the latter; but for one reason or another we do not know very much about the great missionary enterprise of the Irish churches. This is due principally to the fact that, as I have said, the Irish missions were ultimately absorbed by the Roman Church, and we have lost sight of the work of these Irish missionaries because of the greater prominence of their Roman successors. But the story of the missionary pioneers of Ireland is one of thrilling heroism and devotion, second to none that we can read in all the history of the expansion of Christianity.

No one knows who the first Irish Christians were, or who first preached Christianity in that island, or where the first churches were. Possibly Christians from Wales or Britain

---

[1] See Chapter 6.

carried the message to their fellow Celts. More likely the
Gospel came direct from the Continent. Traders from Gaul
and Spain were constantly visiting Ireland, and among these
were without doubt some Christians. Others who were not
traders but simply travellers came to that far-off island, and
as likely as not some of these were Christians. Of course
among these Christian traders or travellers there were those
who were eager to make converts to their faith, to make
Christ known to those who had not heard of Him. So we
can conjecture their telling the wonderful story, giving
Christianity its start in Ireland and so establishing the first
Christian churches. The first definite knowledge we have
of the existence of Irish Christianity is the statement of
Prosper of Aquitaine in his Chronicon under the year 431:
" Palladius having been ordained by Pope Celestine as the
first bishop is sent to the Scots [i. e., Irish] believing in
Christ." But we know little of his work. Apparently he
landed at Wicklow, preached in that neighbourhood for
about a year, founded two or three churches, and then left
Ireland and died in Britain.

This brings us to the great Patrick. Many of the details
of Patrick's life are uncertain, but the chief facts are clear.
Born in Britain, probably in what is now southwestern Scotland, he was trained in a Christian home, his father being a
deacon and his grandfather a priest. When only sixteen
years old he was carried off by a marauding party of Irish
and for six years was a slave in Ireland, tending the swine
of his master. Until then he had given little thought to
religion, but in his misfortune he turned to God, and often
spent long hours at night in prayer in the woods and on the
mountain. That gave him his spiritual training for his
future task. He finally escaped and returned home by way
of the Continent. In response to a vision of the night, in
which he seemed to receive a letter containing " The Voice

of the Irish " and to hear some from their island beseeching him to come and henceforth walk among them, he determined to return to the land of his captivity as a missionary. Either then or before his return home after his escape he spent some years in study in monasteries in Gaul, especially in Auxerre with Germanus, and perhaps at the famous Lerins. In 432, after Palladius had left Ireland and died, Patrick was ordained bishop by Germanus and was sent to Ireland. There for nearly thirty years he gave his life to evangelization. He travelled from one end of the island to the other, preaching the Gospel and establishing churches. Many times he was in peril of his life. Hardships and difficulties filled his days. But he was tireless in his missionary zeal, and he inspired his companions and his converts with his own enthusiasm, with the result that difficulties and opposition were overcome and Christianity was firmly established. It is hardly true to say, as has been said, that " he found no Christians and left no heathen," but he did evangelize Ireland, particularly the northern half. Churches were founded wherever he went, so that thus centres of evangelism were planted widely over the land. Patrick's message was an evangelical one. He knew his Bible thoroughly and used it constantly. In his little *Confession* he quotes from twenty-three books of the New Testament and from ten of the Old.[2] He emphasized the central truths of Christianity and was free from the sacerdotalism that afterwards came to the front. He looked with respect upon the Bishop of Rome, but there is no reliable evidence that he ever visited Rome or that he was ever in any way related to the Pope. He was simply an evangelical of the fifth century, filled with love for Christ and fired with zeal for the preaching of the Gospel. The Roman Catholic Church has

---

[2] White, N. J. D., *St. Patrick—His Writings and Life.*

canonized him as a saint; but he belongs to the whole Church, one of the great Christian pioneers.

During the greater part of the century following Patrick, Christianity in Ireland suffered a spiritual decline. Of the causes we have no certain knowledge, as materials are lacking. We do not even know as much as we need to know about Patrick's work. But it would seem that his work may have been too superficial. He moved rapidly from place to place, preaching the Gospel first to the chiefs and then to others, and wherever there was a favourable response erecting a church or establishing a monastery. Evidence of long-continued residence in these centres is lacking, as is that of thorough training of converts. To be sure, Patrick made a practice of leaving one of his associates at each of the churches he founded, and these carried on the work he had begun. But we know nothing of their work, and we get the impression of a rather constant itineration up and down and across the island. As I have said, some strong Christian centres were established during the thirty years of his residence in Ireland, and these formed the basis of the ecclesiastical organization which he formed, but perhaps too much depended upon one man to make the results as solid and permanent as was desirable. Then again, Patrick had to approach first the king or chief in order to secure land for a church and protection for the Christian disciples. Land belonged not to individuals but to the tribe, and only the chief could assume the right to alienate any of it. The principle of *cujus regio ejus religio* also was universal, and the word of the chief as to the religion of his people was almost decisive. So that Patrick was closely tied up in his work to the chiefs. If they were Christians or maintained their sympathetic support, Christianity would have a strong influence; if they were unfriendly or disinterested the influence would be lessened. A third factor was the lack of strong leaders after Patrick's death in 461.[3] Between that date and the appearing of the great monastic leaders we hear of no strong personalities, except Enda, on the island of Aranmore on the west coast. Without them it was easy for paganism, which still existed widely, to develop again. A further significant reason for the weakening of Christianity may be found in the lack of missionary outreach. In every age spiritual vitality depends upon missionary interest and zeal, and evidence is lacking of missionary work in the period immediately following Patrick. The contrast with the situation in the succeeding monastic period is striking.

We can at best only surmise as to the reasons for the decline of Christianity. It was brought back to new life and zeal by the coming of monasticism from Britain. The monastic movement had found its way from the East into western Europe early in the fourth century, and thence into Britain. Two great monasteries were those at Whithorn in southwestern Scotland and Bangor in north Wales. From these monasticism crossed into Ireland. Finnian went from Ireland to Wales and spent some time at Bangor and other monasteries, and then returned and founded his celebrated monastery at Clonard, some thirty miles west of Dublin, about the year 520. Twenty years or so later another Finnian, who had studied at Whithorn, founded a monastery at Moville, not far from modern Belfast. From these the movement spread rapidly and widely. Famous institutions arose at Clonmacnois, founded by Kieran in 541, at Derry, founded by Columba in 546, at Clonfert, founded by Brendan in 552, at Bangor, founded by Comgall in 558. Others were established at Durrow, Kells, and Glendalough, on many of the islands off the west coast, and elsewhere. Some had only a few monks or nuns, others a large number. Fin-

---

[3] Bury, White, et al., favour this date. Ussher and Todd preferred 493.

nian of Clonard is said to have had 3,000 monks in his monastery at one time. The ecclesiastical system that Patrick had established was no longer in evidence. The monastery was now the dominating factor, the churches founded through the work of the monks being under its care and direction.

As the monasteries rapidly grew in influence and importance, multitudes of young men came to them from all parts of Ireland, being attracted by the opportunity they furnished for cultivation of the spiritual life. The abbots were dominating personalities, and exercised a powerful influence upon the members of the monastic community. The Bible was the centre of interest, and the abbot or prior gave himself to explaining or expounding its truths, especially the Gospels and the Psalms. But other subjects were taught, for the monasteries quickly took on the character of schools. Grammar, rhetoric, geometry, music and Greek were included in the curriculum, all of these being thought of as helpful for the better understanding of the Scriptures and development of the spiritual life—for these were the objects constantly in view. The attention to Greek was noteworthy, for at this time the language was unknown elsewhere in western Europe. As the fame of the monasteries in Ireland spread, earnest young men came to them from over the sea, from England and even from the Continent. From all of this it can be seen what a powerful force the monasteries were in the life of the Irish people, and how it was that religion revived under their leadership.

With the broad outlook and interest which the studies suggest, with the deep spiritual life and devout attitude which was generated, and with the earnest, independent study of the Scriptures, it is not surprising that the monastic schools soon caught the missionary spirit, and became schools of missionary recruiting and training. Young men who came to them became fired with a missionary passion and were eager to go out to preach the Gospel. Out from the monasteries went the monks throughout all Ireland, and the whole nation felt the influence. Then they looked across the water, and soon began to " migrate for Christ." It is significant that some of the abbots themselves undertook missionary service abroad. Columba went to Scotland, Comgall followed him, Brendan took his famous voyage, Fursey went to England and later to France. A zeal for winning the world for Christ gripped the minds and hearts of the monks. Their severe training fitted them for hardship and their constant emphasis upon the unseen world beyond this life cultivated the far look. So the monastery became the great agency for missionary advance, to such an extent that it has been said that " there is no country which in proportion to the extent of its population sent out so many of its sons to serve as missionaries in other European countries." [4] Indeed, as George Smith says, " For eight hundred years Ireland was the missionary school of Christendom in a higher sense than Constantinople or Rome." [5]

The Irish missionary pioneers went first to what is now Scotland. On a clear day one can look across the intervening water, and see Scotland from the Irish shore, so the land to which they went could not have been entirely unknown. As a matter of fact, an Irish colony had been planted in western Scotland early in the fifth century, in what is now Argyllshire. When Columba and a few companions, in 563, went out from their monastery and sailed over to their new mission field it was the beginning of an adventure that was to carry the missionaries of the Irish Church far afield. Indeed, when Columba settled on the little island of Iona, he found a small group of missionaries who had already preceded him. They gave place to him, however, and he estab-

---

[4] Robinson, C. H., *Conversion of Europe*, 46.
[5] *Short History of Christian Missions*, 62.

lished a monastery as the centre of his mission. From this as a base he and his monks went forth into all the country to the north and northeast, and among the people of the many islands off the west coast, preaching the Christian faith and winning large numbers to Christ and Christianity. A visit was made to the Pictish king, Brude, whose capital was near the present Inverness, and he is said to have accepted the new faith. Monasteries were founded in various favourable centres, and these, all subject to Columba, became in their turn bases of evangelism for the people round about. Reinforcements came over from Ireland, and so great a leader as Comgall, abbot of Bangor, visited the new mission and rendered notable service.

At Iona and all the monasteries established by the Irish, the copying of the Scriptures was an outstanding occupation of the monks. There was need for all the copies that could be made, for as we have seen, the monastic schools were centres of Bible study, and naturally the missionaries used the Bible in their work as freely as they had used it as students. So that a portion of time was regularly set apart each day when the more advanced monks copied the Bible, and the scriptorium of the monastery was a busy room. The monks loved the Bible, and gave themselves with a skill that has never been equalled to the embellishment and decoration of the copies which they made. The place which the Bible had in the missionary work of Columba and his successors was notable, growing naturally out of the interest in Bible study in the monasteries of Ireland.

From Scotland the Christian faith spread to England. The British had become pretty well Christianized before the invasions by the Saxons and other pirates from the Continent. An evidence is the presence of three British bishops at the Council of Arles in 314. But the coming of the Saxons, Angles and Jutes, who after raids of increasing frequency definitely established themselves in the second half of the fifth century, made it a heathen land again. The Britons were enslaved, or absorbed, or driven back into the west or the north of the island, or were destroyed. So that England was again a field for missionary service.

In the year that Columba died—597—Augustine, sent from Rome, landed in Kent and began once more the preaching of the Christian Gospel. Neither he nor his immediate followers had great success. Kent accepted Christianity, and a beginning was made among the East Saxons and in Northumbria. However, in neither of these last two kingdoms did Christianity gain much more of a place than the nominal acceptance of it by the ruler, and when a new king came into power who was not a Christian the land became heathen again.

Oswald, Christian king of Northumbria, when he came to the throne in 634, found England a heathen country except for Kent, a few Christians in his own kingdom, and the Britons on the Welsh border and in the northwest. That England became Christian is due to his action in bringing Irish missionaries in from Iona. He had spent some time at Iona when in exile from Northumbria and had there been baptized and received Christian training, so it was natural that he should turn to that centre when he sought missionaries for his country, rather than to the Roman mission in Kent, a foreign kingdom. After an inauspicious beginning by a bishop named Corman, Aidan came from Iona into Northumbria, and established as the centre of his work a monastery on the island of Lindisfarne, now called Holy Island. Aidan was not alone in his work. King Oswald himself engaged in missionary effort, heartily supporting his bishop and not infrequently interpreting for him, since evidently he knew but little of the Anglian tongue. Moreover, as Bede tells us,[6] " many from the country of the Scots

---

[6] *Hist. Eccles.*, iii, 3. [7] IV, p. 88.

began to come daily into Britain, and with great devotion preached the word of faith." These and English youths whom Aidan and his successors trained went during the succeeding decades throughout Northumbria, Mercia, Essex, as well as more remote sections, and definitely won the land for Christ and the Christian faith. It was not Augustine and his companions, missionaries of Rome, who made England Christian, though they began the work; but the Irish missionaries from Iona or direct from Ireland. Montalembert, the Roman Catholic author of *The Monks of the West*, says, " What is distinctly visible is the influence of Celtic priests and missionaries everywhere replacing, or seconding, the Roman missionaries and reaching districts which their predecessors had never been able to enter. The stream of the divine Word thus extended itself from north to south, and its slow but certain course reached in succession all the people of the heptarchy." [7] When English Christianity came later into fellowship with Rome the Irish influence still persisted,[8] and the direction originally given to English life by the Irish missionaries became a permanent possession, to give it the characteristics which it has since had.

Shortly after Columba began his missionary work in what we know as Scotland others in the Irish monasteries began to look farther. In 673 Columbanus with twelve companions bade their fellow-students good-bye and set sail for the Continent. They were the first in a long succession of missionaries from Ireland who were to make the Irish name well known on the Continent, as they carried the Gospel into the lands of western and central Europe. Outstanding among them all was Columbanus. It would seem that he and his Irish companions spent some time in Brittany on landing on the Continent, quite natural in view of the Celtic

[8] Meissner, J. L. G., *The Celtic Church in Britain After the Synod of Whitby.*

people who inhabited that peninsula, especially the Britons who had crossed over from their own land to escape the Saxon invaders. Many of these were Christians, and Columbanus strengthened their faith and preached to those who had not accepted Christ. He took with him some of the Breton young men as associates in his work in France. His great centre of work was his monastery at Luxeuil in eastern France. At least 105 monastic centres in eastern and northern France grew out of his original foundation or accepted the rule which he established in his monasteries.

Others besides Columbanus and his followers also went to France with the Gospel. A notable name is that of Fursey. He was an Irish monk who had evangelized western Ireland from his monastery on Lough Corrib, then had gone to England and done outstanding service in Christianizing East Anglia, and finally moved on to France about the year 648. This was nearly sixty years after Columbanus began his mission there, a fact which reminds us that the effort on the part of the Irish Church to Christianize the people of the Continent was a long-continued one. In fact, for two centuries there was a steady stream of missionaries moving across from Ireland to France and other continental countries. Fursey was one of these. He worked in northern France, on the border of Belgium, and then at Lagny, near Paris. His name is said to be met with in connection with large numbers of shrines and other memorials, evidence of the substantial character of his mission.

Again led by Columbanus the Irish missionary movement spread into what is now Germany and Switzerland. In Switzerland the work begun by Columbanus was continued by his disciple and associate Gall, and we have a permanent memorial of his mission in the city of St. Gall, built where he had his monk's cell. The monastery which later succeeded this became one of the principal seats of learning on the Continent, and a notable centre for students and missionaries from Ireland. Others after Gall and Columbanus continued the work of preaching the Gospel in Switzerland and Germany, laying foundations upon which in large measure the Christian life of those lands was built. We have evidence of the strength of their work and influence in the bitter opposition of Boniface in the eighth century, one of whose principal objectives was to drive out the Irish missionaries and to bring their followers into the Roman fold.

Italy must also be mentioned, for on the slopes of the Apennines Columbanus founded a third centre of missionary endeavour, at Bobbio, afterwards famous for its great collection of valuable manuscripts. Here effort went on for the conversion of the pagans and the winning of the Arian Lombards to the orthodox faith.

Thus in many parts of the countries of western and southern Europe—the places I have mentioned are only illustrations—the Irish missionary movement appeared. The story quite justifies the estimate I have quoted as to the importance of the Irish in the Christianizing of Europe. The missionaries brought their own characteristic ideas and methods. They held fast to their traditions, made their monasteries centres of learning, stressed purity of life, insisted on independence from authority whether of the civil government or of Rome. Ultimately causes to which reference is made later led to the absorption of their work by the Roman Church, but they made an imperishable contribution to the Christianizing of both the British Isles and the continental lands.

I

There were giants in this missionary enterprise of the Irish Christians. Some of them I have mentioned. They deserve closer study. But only brief reference to a few can be made.

The first of the great names is Enda. He was the son of

the king of the Oriels in Ulster, and on the death of his father was chosen to succeed him. It is a graphic story how, after leading his soldiers in triumphant conflicts with his many enemies, the doughty warrior came one day to the monastic house presided over by his sister, and there was converted to Christ. Not long afterward he crossed over to what is now Scotland and took a course of training at Ninian's famous monastery of Candida Casa, or Whithorn, and then spent a brief time in Rome. Coming back to his native Ireland, he preached and founded churches in the eastern part of the country, and finally secured from the king of Cashel, who ruled the south and west, the grant of the island of Inishmore, or Aranmore, largest of the Aran Islands off the coast of Galway. Here he built monasteries, and gathered a group of students around him, not many in number but of choice quality. For here were trained such great Christian leaders as Kieran of Clonmacnois, Brendan of Clonfert, Finnian of Moville, and most notable of all, Columba. No wonder that many other devoted youth flocked to Enda's island monastery, and that the island became known as Aran-na-naomh, "Aran of the Saints." Enda was the herald of the dawn, for when he died, about 542, the new day had just broken in the Christian history of Ireland after the night of reaction following Patrick's great work. Many factors made him what he became, and one of these was the influence of his sister. She had a strong power over him from the day of his conversion; she directed his training and study; it was she who went to Rome to bring him back to Ireland and to his great work there. Enda's influence was very wide. Of what quality it was, and of what depth and breadth his character must have been, is evident from the names of those who studied under his leadership and inspired by him went out to be missionaries for Christ in Ireland and beyond the seas.

Finnian, the founder of the monastic school at Clonard in central Ireland, was another of the early giants. As a youth, he sought deeper insight into the truths of Scripture, and for this purpose went to Wales and studied a long time under St. David and other Welsh monastic teachers. On his return to Ireland he founded Clonard. To this centre came great throngs of young men—three thousand, so we are told, though that figure is open to suspicion, it is so common in the story of other monasteries. But, at any rate, we have Archbishop Ussher as authority for the statement that scholars came out of Clonard " in as great numbers as Greeks of old from the sides of the horse of Troy." [9] Finnian was known as the preceptor of " the twelve apostles of Ireland," from a group of outstanding Christian leaders who studied with him, among whom were Columba, Comgall and Kieran (Ciaran) of Clonmacnois. Of other work done by him we know little, but to be the teacher of great evangelists and missionaries like those mentioned is to have a place of eminence in Irish Christian history that might well be envied.

In any list of the early Christian leaders of Ireland the name of Comgall must appear. He was not a Scot,[10] like Finnian, Columba and the other leaders of the Church, but a Pict, from the colony established in northeastern Ireland by that people. After his studies with Finnian of Clonard and others he was ordained at Clonmacnois, and eagerly planned to cross the seas to Britain, but was persuaded to remain in Ireland. At Bangor, on Belfast Lough, he built his monastery, and multitudes came to it from every quarter. Among them was Columbanus, most famous of his disciples. The distinctive characteristic of the rule which he

---

[9] *Dictionary of Christian Biography*, ii, 518.
[10] In early centuries the Irish were known as Scots, and gave their name to Scotland when the leader of their colonists there became king of the country.

established was its severity. To the usual rule of prayer, manual work and the reading of Scripture he added fasting. So severe was the asceticism demanded by him that seven monks are said to have died of cold and hunger, and he was urged to relax the severity of his rule, but he refused. It was this intense and abnormal asceticism that Columbanus carried to France. In spite of the severity of life in his monastery it gained rather than lost in popularity, due probably to the high standard of educational training given there, and the aggressive spirit of Christian service that was fostered, which naturally appealed to red-blooded young men. He taught them to be " soldiers for Christ," and they followed his teaching. And he set them an example as well, for he himself finally crossed the sea as a missionary, joining Columba in Scotland for a time, founding a monastic centre on Tiree, and accompanying Columba on his visit to Brude, king of the Picts, his knowledge of the Pictish language and the fact that he himself was a Pict proving valuable factors in winning that ruler to the Christian faith. Comgall, like Columba, was intense in feeling, but tremendously in earnest in his devotion to his Master. He was a scholarly teacher, an aggressive leader, a skilful administrator; and his monastic school at Bangor, with the Welsh Bangor on the Dee, and Columba's Iona, were " the three great lights of Celtic Christianity." [11]

A host of other names crowd forward for attention. That of Brigid (Bridget, Bride) surely deserves mention. At least eight early biographies of her are known. She flourished around the end of the fifth century, and her monastic home in Kildare became the centre and head of a system of widely-scattered monasteries for both men and women, who were trained under her leadership for Christian service and evangelism. She was a woman of great Christian devotion,

[11] *Dictionary of Christian Biography,* i, 609.

and her charity and piety and love for the Scriptures made her an outstanding figure in the days when the Irish Church was gathering its strength for its great missionary task.

Brendan the Traveller, abbot of Clonfert, must also be mentioned. He was one of the so-called " twelve apostles of Ireland," and founded churches not only in Ireland but in Scotland and Britain as well. In search of the Land of Promise he set sail on a long seven years' voyage, which carried him far to the west and north, preaching the Gospel and establishing many Christian centres. But the most famous place connected with his name was his monastery at Clonfert. A beautiful story is told of the heavenly music he heard from the altar of his church, and how after hearing it he never cared again for earthly music. He died in 577, having not only trained many for evangelistic and missionary service but by his travels having set an example of pioneering which became a tradition in the Church.

Of the leaders in the conversion of Scotland and England, Columba ranks first. I must say more of him. We wish that we had more information about him and that the information we do have were more trustworthy. There is an old Irish life whose author we do not know, and there is a life by Adamnan, the fifth successor of Columba as abbot of Iona. The latter is our chief authority. But, like all the early lives of saints, it is really a legendary rather than a biography, presenting what was supposed to be spiritually helpful instead of a full and critical account of the life. Thus Adamnan divided his life of Columba into three parts, prophecies, miracles, and visions. But while important things are missing we can get a fairly clear picture of the great Irish missionary.

Columba was born in County Donegal, being descended on both sides from royal families. He studied with Enda on Inishmore, with Finnian at Moville, and also with Finnian of Clonard. After his ordination as a Christian minister he spent fifteen years in Ireland, establishing churches and founding monasteries in various parts of the country, among the latter Derry and Durrow. He was forty-two years old when he set out across the sea with twelve companions for the land that could dimly be seen from the northeastern Irish shore, and at Iona began the wide-ranging work for the Picts and Scots of which I have spoken above, and which he carried on for thirty-four years until his death in 597. Bede says " he converted the Pictish nation to the faith of Christ by his preaching and example." [12] Evidently, then, he was an effective preacher, even though occasionally he had to speak through an interpreter. Doubtless his effectiveness was due in not a little measure to his use of the Bible. This may be noted as a characteristic of the man. He loved the Word of God, and was copying the thirty-fourth Psalm on the very last night of his life. The intensity of his earnestness was another quality that made him a good preacher. The doubtful story of the war against the king to which he is said to have incited his followers, and in expiation of which grave sin he was advised to exchange Ireland for the mission field, and the later story of the battle between his followers and those of Comgall, tell of a vehemence of spirit that was apparently characteristic of him, whatever may be the truth as to the contests themselves. Bede, who looked with abhorrence upon the Irish Church and its methods, but who nevertheless appreciated the Christian character of many of its leaders, would have us know that Columba's example was a potent factor in the winning of the people to Christianity. Columba was sympathetic. A beautiful story is told of how the Iona monks, returning wearied from the harvest field, for several days

[12] *Hist. Eccles.*, iii, 4.

felt a strange influence that wondrously uplifted and gladdened them, and how Baithen, the senior monk, explained to
them that Columba, mindful of their toil, was thinking
anxiously about them and was grieving that they had so
long a day of work, and as he could not go in body to meet
them his spirit met their steps and consoled them and made
them glad.[13] Such was the attention he gave to prayer. All
the monks spent stated periods in prayer, but the story I
have just quoted shows that prayer was something vital with
Columba and not simply a formality. He was a lover of
nature, too. He could hardly have lived for a generation in
the midst of the scenery of the western islands and the
northern highlands without having their beauty sink deep
into his soul. As Bishop Lightfoot says, " Columba loved
men and he loved nature because in both he saw God." [14]
He was a man of humility, like his Master bathing the feet
of His brethren. He set a constant example of industry, to
such an extent that " he could not pass the space even of a
single hour without applying himself either to prayer, or
reading, or writing, or else to some manual labour." [15] He
was not so serious and austere but that he could always have,
as Bede tells us, a pleasant, holy countenance. And Lightfoot sums up his character when he says that " his vision
embraced the great spiritual realities of life. He regarded
things with a spiritual eye." Here was the source of his
power. " He was gladdened in his inmost heart by the joy
of the Holy Spirit." It is no wonder that his followers for
centuries looked back to him as to an apostle of Christ.

Of Columba's followers none was more important than
Aidan, whose great work in the conversion of England I
have mentioned. He was of noble birth, the son of an Irish

---

[13] Adamnan, *Life of Columba,* i, 29.
[14] *Leaders in the Northern Church,* App., 183.
[15] Adamnan, *op. cit.,* i, 2nd pref.

saint commemorated in the calendar, and was in the same line as St. Brigid. He was not unworthy of his ancestors, for when Corman reported to an assembly of the monks at Iona his unsuccessful mission to England, it is said that the whole assembly recognized in Aidan the one who should go to England in his place. Aidan's success was due in part to the hearty co-operation of the king, Oswald, but largely to his own outstanding qualities. Bede, who " very much detested " his teaching as to the time for observing Easter, speaks with enthusiasm of those qualities, and tells us of his assiduous devotion to the preaching of the Gospel. He went throughout Northumbria (from the Firth of Forth to the River Humber), usually accompanied by some of his fellow-monks or by the king, preaching and talking with the people. The monastery which he established on the island of Lindisfarne became what we may think of as the first theological seminary on English soil, for according to Irish custom it was a centre of learning and of training for evangelism and missionary service. Early in his ministry he selected twelve youths " to be instructed in Christ," [16] who were followed by others either English or Irish. It was this wise custom of his that made possible the wide spread of the message and the Christianizing of the greater part of England by him and his followers. Aidan held to the ascetic ideal which was characteristic of the Irish monks. Bede speaks of his " diligence in reading and watchings," [17] and even when he was invited to eat with his friend the king he ate very sparingly and hurried off to his nearby monastery to engage in the reading of the Bible or in prayer. Several miracles are supposed to have been wrought by his prayers, a tradition which is a sufficient testimony to the reputation he bore as a prayerful man. Differing, perhaps, from his great master Co-

[16] Bede, *Hist. Eccles.*, iii, 26. [17] *Op. cit.*, iii, 17.

lumba, he was a man of irenic disposition, and in spite of his asceticism was genial and friendly, a trait without which he could not possibly have achieved such success in winning the people to the new faith.

Aidan was generous. He had no possessions but his island home, but he frequently received gifts of money from the rich, and these he always distributed to the poor or used in ransoming slaves. His broad spirit and his insight are seen in the fact that he recognized the part which women could play in the evangelization of the people, and in line with this he consecrated the first woman Christian leader in northern England, Heiu, who became the founder of the monastery of Hartlepool; more significant was his inspiring Hilda to take her great place in Christian education and leadership. Bishop Lightfoot sums up Aidan's qualities in the statement that " he had all the virtues of his Celtic race without any of its faults," perhaps a rather exaggerated estimate. But he supports his claim by a comparison of him with Columba, as also with Augustine, Wilfrid and Cuthbert. He was eminent, he points out, in " the singular sweetness and breadth and sympathy of his character." [18]

Aidan the missionary, Oswald the king, and Hilda the educator were the three great leaders in the Christianizing of northern and eastern England. With Hilda are to be mentioned some of those whom Aidan trained, such as Chad (Ceadda), Cedd (Cedda), and Eata. Hilda was in the royal line of Northumbria from King Edwin, and was baptized by Paulinus, the early Roman bishop in that kingdom. After Aidan began his work she came under his influence, and was set apart to Christian service. She was abbess of Hartlepool after Heiu, and in 657 founded her famous abbey at Whitby, which until her death in 680 was a centre of Christian learn-

[18] *Leaders in the Northern Church,* 44.

ing and missionary evangelism. She was evidently a woman
of outstanding ability as an organizer and administrator.
Robinson says that " to her initiative was largely due the
development of the monasteries which became centres of
education in the north of England." [19] Whitby was a double
monastery, that is, it contained both men and women. A
notable figure among its monks was Caedmon, the father of
English poetry. At Whitby Hilda established a strict rule,
with rigid observance of the usual virtues of piety, chastity
and poverty, but emphasizing especially peace and love.
This suggests another side to her character quite as important as her administrative ability. She was a woman of
" singular piety and grace, . . . a pattern of life." [20] Bede
speaks of her industry and virtue. She held to the customs
of the Celtic mission, even after the decision of the Synod of
Whitby had turned the scales in favour of the Roman side,
and steadfastly opposed Wilfrid. It is clear from this and
from her close relation to Aidan that she held to the spiritual
ideals of the Irish. It is equally clear from her acceptance
of the Whitby decision that her emphasis upon peace and
love was no nominal thing. It is said that on the last night
of her life she gathered her nuns around her and exhorted
them to keep the peace among themselves and with others.[20]
Kings and princes came to her for advice, and she trained
her pupils so well in the Scriptures that many of them became leaders in the Church, five of them bishops. Hilda
well deserves the place she holds in the history of Christianity in England.

Among the young men whom Aidan trained in his monastery on Lindisfarne were the two brothers Cedd and Chad.
They belonged to a remarkable Anglian family, for not only
did these two attain eminence in the Church but they had

---

[19] *Conversion of Europe*, 135.   [20] Bede, *Hist. Eccles.*, iv, 23.

two brothers [21] who were among the clergy, Caelin, chaplain of King Oidilwald of Deira, and Cynibill. Cedd and Chad both became bishops. Cedd was born in Northumbria, and assisted Aidan in his missionary work in northern England, as well as doubtless Finan who succeeded him. On the baptism of Peada, son of the Mercian king Penda, Cedd was one of four monks who went back with him to South Anglia, which he ruled under his father. When Sigbert, king of Essex, accepted Christianity and asked for Christian teachers, Cedd was recalled by King Oswy of Northumbria and sent with a companion to Essex. In Mercia he had won many to the faith, especially among the nobles. In his new field he was quite as successful, and was consecrated Bishop of the East Saxons by Finan. There he worked for some years, establishing many churches. In his home country of Northumbria he also built a monastery, not far from Whitby —his brother Cynibill finishing it when he himself had to return to Essex. At the Synod of Whitby, in 664, he took the Irish side, true to his teachers Aidan and Finan. Bede says that he was moderator of the synod. When the king's decision went against the Irish, however, he accepted the Roman custom as to the time for the observance of Easter, the chief question at issue. Shortly after the meeting of the synod he died of the plague at his monastery. Cedd seems to have been a man of irenic spirit, though he could speak straight out to the king when the latter's conduct appeared to merit reproof. He followed the simple manner of life characteristic of the Irish monks, going about on foot among the cottages and castles in the country and preaching the Gospel to the people in the towns. Bede says that in South Anglia he " diligently preached the Word," and we can believe that he did so in Essex and Northumbria.

----

[21] Howorth, H. H., *Golden Days of the Early English Church*, i, 141. See also ii, 50.

Chad, Cedd's brother, received the latter's monastery from him by bequest upon his death. After King Oswy's son Alchfrid had irregularly appointed Wilfrid to the bishopric of York, Oswy appointed Chad Bishop of the Northumbrians with his seat at York, and he was ordained by Wini, Bishop of the West Saxons, as there was no other bishop nearer. He continued in York for only a brief period, for King Egfrid, who succeeded Oswy in Northumbria, removed him and put Wilfrid in his place. Shortly, however, King Wulfhere of Mercia appealed to Theodore at Canterbury to appoint a bishop for his people, and Chad was appointed, fixing his episcopal see at Lichfield, where he served all of central England for seven years, until his death in 672. Until Whitby, Chad had maintained the Irish position in regard to the time of Easter, but he accepted the new situation, while retaining otherwise the Irish customs and rule. Bede speaks of " his many merits of continence, humility, teaching, prayers, voluntary poverty, and other virtues." [22] It was perhaps a questionable humility when he submitted to reconsecration as bishop by Theodore. But his fine spirit appears in his words: " I never thought myself worthy of it, but though unworthy, I submitted to undertake it in obedience to authority " [23]—referring to his original acceptance of the office. When his last day came and he had gathered his monks around him, he " admonished them to preserve the virtues of love and peace among themselves and toward all others." [24] Like his brother Cedd, he seems to have been of sweet and peace-loving disposition, faithful in his ministry according to the ideals of the Irish missionaries who had preceded him, and able in his administration of his great episcopal field. These two brothers are but eminent illustrations of a large group of missionaries of the Irish Church in Eng-

---

[22] *Hist. Eccles.*, iv, 3.   [23] *Ibid.*, iv, 2.   [24] *Ibid.*, iv, 3.

land who were not foreigners like Aidan and Finan and Colman, but were native Englishmen, or Anglians. To them, with their great leaders from Iona, was due the Christianizing of most of England.

We have seen how Christianity through the work of the Irish missionaries spread not only to Scotland and England but to the Continent. In this part of the story the greatest name is Columbanus. Basically, his name is the same as Columba's, and indeed he is not infrequently called Columba in some of the codices of his life. He is worthy to rank with the great Columba of Iona, with whom he was in part a contemporary. Columbanus was born in Leinster, and, according to Jonas, his biographer, insidious temptations early in life led him to turn his attention to the safety of religion, and he gave himself with great exertion ("sweat" is the expressive word used by Jonas) to the study of grammar, rhetoric, geometry and the Scriptures. Going one day to visit a woman who was a hermit, he was challenged by her to do what she herself had been unable to do, cross the sea as a pilgrim for Christ. He resolved to follow her counsel, but his mother was overcome at the thought of his leaving her, and threw herself on the floor across the doorway. His vision called him, however, and he stepped across her prostrate body to go "wherever the way of salvation should open a road." [25] After a short time spent with a highly esteemed Bible student and teacher Sinil he made his way to Bangor, where the famous Comgall had his great monastic school. He passed many years there, studying and teaching and working, but the words of the old recluse could not be forgotten, and he sought Comgall's approval of a foreign mission. He had become so indispensable to Comgall that it was with difficulty that the abbot could bring himself to

---

[25] Jonas, *Life of Columbanus*, i, 3.

favour his going. But finally he gave him his blessing, and Columbanus, with twelve companions, like the Lord and His twelve apostles, set sail one day from Ireland, never to return.

We have in this story of his early life the key to his later attitude and achievements. His unwavering devotion to what he believed to be right, his persistence in following his purpose, his thoroughness and careful attention to detail, his own scholarliness and the standard of learning which he set before the Christian leaders of Gaul—all of these had their springs in the early experiences of his life and his years of training under Comgall. From the latter he received the intense ascetic tendencies which made his rule so rigorous and so unnatural, and which led in the end to the substitution of the more human Benedictine rule in many of his monasteries. He was unflinching in his denunciation of evil wherever he found it, and the picture of the Christian monk facing the Frankish king and confronting him with his egregious sins is a stirring and stimulating one. He showed the same fearlessness in his condemnation of the base paganism of the Alemanni of Switzerland. He was not always tactful, but could never be charged with weakness. In line with the loose independence which characterized the Irish organization he had no relations with the bishops of Gaul and did not recognize their authority nor follow their customs. This led them to call a synod and to summon him to come and explain himself. Nothing shows better the independence, tact and humility which were combined in him than his letter of reply: " I pray you through our common Lord . . . that I be permitted to dwell, with your peace and charity, in these forests, and to live beside the bones of my seventeen departed brethren. And we will pray for you, as we have done until now, and as we ought to do. Let Gaul receive together those whom the kingdom of heaven will receive, if we are deserving

of good. . . . Let us not quarrel with one another. . . .
Pray for us, my fathers, even as we, humble as we are, pray
for you. Regard us not as strangers, for we are members
together of one body. . . . Therefore let us all rejoice in the
knowledge of the faith and the revelation of the Son of God
. . . in communion with Whom let us learn to love one another and pray for one another." [26]

He was quite as tactfully bold in writing to Pope Gregory
and Pope Boniface. On the other hand, he could use strong
terms in his condemnation of those who opposed his preaching. He was constantly a Bible student, as appears not only
from his expositions of the Psalms, but also from his sermons and epistles. He was tireless in preaching the Gospel,
possessing a magnetic personality that attracted large numbers to his monasteries, and able in addition to all his other
activities to organize and administer not one but three monasteries and to direct his followers in their monastic work.
Through all his days he was the master missionary, looking
with longing toward the unreached peoples beyond, and even
at the sunset of his life pressing on to new fields with the
evangel that in his earliest years had won him, the evangel
that through all the decades of crowded endeavour had
dominated his thought and effort.

Among the companions of Columbanus was Gall, whom I
have mentioned. He was one of the original twelve who had
been at Bangor with Columbanus and with him had gone
forth on the mission to the Continent. He seems to have
been a good linguist, and was able to preach not only in
Latin but in the language of the Alemanni, thus making himself indispensable to his leader Columbanus, as the latter
could not speak to the people except through an interpreter.
He loved to fish, and enjoyed the woods and the hills. These

---

[26] *Epis. ii*, in Migne, lxxx. col. 264ff.

human characteristics were invaluable, for when Columbanus antagonized the people and found it necessary to leave the country, Gall stayed behind and gained an increasing place of influence among the inhabitants. Near the southern shore of Lake Constance, where the city of St. Gall now stands, he built his cell, and there he lived for many years, preaching to the people and teaching them the things of God. He was urged by the monks of Luxeuil, where he and his master had lived and laboured so long, to become their abbot, but he refused. The duke of the Alemanni would have appointed him bishop of his people, but this honour also he declined. Gall was not a man for the complexities of administration or the distractions of official life. Rather his strength was to be found in the less prominent but equally effective ministry of the simple life, the quiet service of personal relationship, the teaching of those who might come to his cell or the preaching to those whom he could gather together here and there as he travelled about the country. But his influence was widespread, and " when he died, in 646,[27] the whole country inhabited by the Alemanni had become Christian." [28]

I have mentioned Fursey, an Irish missionary who worked quite independently of Columbanus and his disciples, one of a considerable company of such independent missionaries who made their way to the Continent on their " pilgrimage for Christ." Fursey was born in Munster of noble heritage in the early part of the seventh century. He lived for a time in the monastery of Meldan on Inchiquin in Lough Corrib. Possibly he also built himself a monastery on that island. Later he had an oratory near Cong, at the northern end of the lake, a larger church near Headford, not far from the eastern shore, and a monastery a short distance away. This was all part of a wide ministry in Ireland. He had many

[27] Some authorities say 629.
[28] Robinson, *Conversion of Europe*, 317.

visions, doubtless brought on by his extreme ascetic life, and these he used in his missionary journeys through Ireland and later Scotland. They have been thought to be, in part at least, the basis for those which Dante describes in his *Divine Comedy*. About 633 he went to England and settled in East Anglia. Here, near what is now Yarmouth, he founded a monastery within the remains of an old Roman fort (Burgcastle). He had come to England partly to escape the crowds that came to him in Ireland, and in his English monastery he sought quiet that " he might with more freedom indulge his heavenly studies." [29] But he could not or would not give up his practice of preaching the Gospel, and " by the example of his virtue and the efficacy of his discourse he converted the unbelievers to Christ, and confirmed in the faith and love of Christ those who already believed." [29] Desiring, however, a more complete withdrawal from the influences of the world, he turned over his monastery to his brother Fullan, retired to a cell where Ultan, another brother, lived, and there for a while devoted himself to prayer and meditation. But after a time, as has been said, his missionary eagerness called him back into active service and carried him across the Channel to France. Peronne and Lagny are the two places most noteworthy in his missionary story, but they are only two among very many. After a life of wideranging missionary service he died in France about 650.

Bede tells us that Fursey had from earliest days applied himself to the reading of sacred books. Evidently he shared the universal Irish eagerness for learning. His visions or dreams were most fantastic, but they show that his thoughts were fixed upon spiritual things and the life in the angelic world. Yet he did not lose himself in other-worldliness; he kept in touch with his fellowmen and their needs and gave

---

[29] Bede, *Hist. Eccles.*, iii, 19.

himself without reserve to the preaching of the Gospel which he knew they needed. It is a testimony to the dominant missionary purpose, characteristic not only of Fursey but of the Irish Christian leaders generally, that though he tried to pull himself away from an active life and devote himself to self-cultivation, he could not resist the pull in another direction and soon found himself back in missionary service again. Like Chad, he was one of a family of brothers who were eminent missionaries. Fullan, to whom he turned over his monastery at Burgcastle, followed him to France and built a monastery near Mons and finally is said to have won a martyr's crown. Ultan also went on a mission to France, and became abbot of Fosse and later of Peronne.

These are but a few of the giants in the Irish missionary enterprise. Other names we know, but the names of very many are unknown to us. They formed a great company of missionary pioneers, carrying the evangel through Ireland, across to Scotland, down into England, and finally to the Continent, leaving to us the inspiration of their noble character and devoted service, and contributing richly to the Christian world enterprise of today in the wise methods and enduring principles which we can learn from them for our work.

II

What were the achievements of the Irish missions? And what enduring results are to be chronicled? Most noteworthy, of course, were the followers they gained in the many lands where the missionaries were at work, the converts they won to Christ, the Christian churches they established. One cannot guess the number of those whom they gained for the faith. That it was immense we can readily see from the wide spread of their work, the long lists of churches and monasteries which can be catalogued, the in-

fluential position held by many of their Christian centres and
many of their leaders, and the fact that through them Christianity came to dominate the peoples whom they evangelized.
Even if the results had not lasted beyond their own lives, the
work of the Irish missionaries would be counted successful in
high degree. To win individual Irishmen, or Picts, or Anglians, or Franks to Christ the Saviour was their chief and primary aim. There could be none higher. And in this they
were outstanding. As evangelists, they won a place of eminence for all time in Christian history, and through eternal
ages a great company whom no man can number will give
thanks to God for these who brought them the knowledge of
Christ and led them from darkness into the light.

The achievements of the Irish missionaries in personal
evangelism are thus plainly evident. That there were enduring results in the national life may not be so clear at first
glance. But when we point out that through their labours
Christianity was permanently established in the lands where
they wrought, it will be seen that they set in motion forces
that continued after their missions had come to an end, and
that they introduced into the life of the peoples an element that was to be abiding. On the one hand, there was
the Christian life and experience. To be sure, it was not a
Christianity of the highest quality, even during the lifetime
of the missionaries themselves, and through the centuries
since then there have been periods when the Christianity of
the people sank to a very low level. But it must be remembered that they were laying foundations; Christianity was
only at its beginning with these peoples. And if the development in future years was not all that one could wish—well,
we ourselves have not yet developed our Christianity perfectly. The missionaries gave the best that they had and did
their work well, so well that Christianity never afterwards
was lost from the life of the people. The Irish mission-

ary movement itself disappeared. The Roman Church took the place of the Irish, and later the Roman gave way to the Protestant. " One soweth and another reapeth." But the reaping would be impossible without the sowing, and those who reap depend on those who sow. It is simple historical fact that the sowing was done by the Irish missionaries, and that they did their work so well that Christianity was permanently settled in the lands which they evangelized, so that the Christian movement has never been lost out of them.

Consider also the Christian Church, the organized embodiment of the Christian life. There were striking differences between the Irish Church and the Roman which succeeded it. The Irish Church was independent of any central authority; the Roman owned allegiance to the Pope. The Irish Church was loosely organized, the several groups having scarcely closer relation to one another than the groups of Protestantism in later centuries or today; on the other hand, the Roman was developing its hierarchy of priests, bishops and archbishops, with all sections of the Church increasingly integrated into a well-organized ecclesiastical body. The Irish Church, though it had bishops, was organized around the monastery, whose head was often simply a presbyter; the Roman emphasized the bishop and rapidly developed the diocesan plan. The differences between Irish and Roman churches, however, were hardly greater than those between the Church in general in the seventh century and that today. The early Church was monastic, whatever its ecclesiastical connection; today monks and nuns, even in the Catholic churches, are of quite secondary importance and the Church has a secular organization. The differences are especially noteworthy when one considers the Protestant churches of today. The free churches of England are certainly in a true succession from the Irish Church of the seventh century, but though the message is not essentially different the whole method and dominating idea is worlds removed from the method and idea of the earlier time. Through all these changes, however, the Church has lasted on, building on the foundation laid by the missionaries of the Irish Christian faith. Forms have changed, authority has changed, ecclesiastical ideas have changed, yet the Church established by the Irish pioneers still goes on, in lineal succession through the centuries. One is handicapped in the study of the Irish Church by the fact that the churches which have succeeded it have been dominantly those of a closely organized episcopal order, and that the historians of the Irish Church have been almost uniformly from the Anglican or Roman Church. It would be breaking almost entirely new ground to consider the Irish Church from the point of view of the free churches. Perhaps we shall yet find in the organization and life of these early churches more of value than we have believed. But the great fact is that in whatever form the Church is to be found in the lands where the Irish missionaries worked, the Church of today is the successor of the Irish. The Church established by them still exists, even though in other forms.

If the Irish missions achieved all this, it is fair to ask, Why did they not continue? How is it that the Roman Church succeeded in absorbing the Irish churches into its system and ultimately wiping out the independent Irish movement altogether? There is no entirely satisfactory answer, but several causes are clear.

In the first place, there was the power of the Roman organization. Its strength was a gradual growth. In the sixth century the Pope had little authority beyond the Alps, and was scarcely thought of as more than the senior bishop, to be honoured but by no means to be obeyed unless his injunctions approved themselves to local authorities. In England (except in Kent) and in Scotland and Ireland, the Church was entirely autonomous until near the end of the seventh century. With the appointment of Theodore as Archbishop of Canterbury, however, papal authority gained recognition in the British Isles, and at the same time increased papal power developed on the Continent; Iona became divided in its allegiance and Lindisfarne yielded to Roman jurisdiction, and the Frankish bishops loyally obeyed the behests of Boniface the Roman archbishop. The strength of the developing hierarchy was put behind the effort to bring all Christians into conformity to Rome, and the missionaries and other leaders devoted themselves quite as assiduously to destroying what they termed heresy as to winning to the Christian faith those who were still pagan. Civil rulers were influenced increasingly by ecclesiastical organization, just as today " princes of the Church," and bishops in communions episcopally organized, secure attention from civil authorities which it is often difficult for leaders of other churches to gain. And the Roman Church used this advantage to the full. The power of the organization was made possible largely by the wise choice of strong men for places of large and outstanding leadership. To mention only two such leaders—though these were the most important ones, to be sure—Theodore in England and Boniface in Germany personified the power of Rome and its imperial policy, and to their ability was largely due the weakening of the Irish influence and the absorption of the Irish missions by Rome.

There was a steady development of sacerdotalism in the Irish Church, and this was a second cause of the disappearance of Church and missions into Rome. In the days of Patrick there was very little of this. Irish Christianity was just about what was to be found in Gaul, though somewhat more simplified owing to its primitive character, and more independent due to its isolation. Judged by twentieth century standards, Patrick was a pretty heretical Catholic. His writings show him to have been evangelical rather than sacerdotal in his attitude. Christ and His Gospel were primary. It is of these that he speaks. The efficacy of the Church and its ordinances is quite in the background. When the Irish missionaries began to go forth in the sixth century, the evangelical spirit was still to the fore, and the attitude and message which was characteristic of them I have already described in speaking of certain of the leaders. But even thus early the sacerdotal element is to be seen, the growing prominence of the mass, the emphasis upon other service forms and priestly functions, the use of the sign of the cross, etc. Though we must remember that practically all we know of the Irish missionaries and their work comes to us through followers of the Roman faith; how much of their own customs they read into the history of the Irish cause we do not know. Doubtless the emphasis upon the miraculous which was involved in this growing sacerdotal attitude was stimulated by the widespread, apparently universal, belief in supernatural powers, visions, miracles and wonders that seems to us almost incredible. At any rate, sacerdotalism to some extent developed in the Irish Church, until its message was apparently not radically different from that of the Roman Church. Naturally, that weakened its independence and made it easier for Rome to gain the supremacy. Moreover, its strength had rested upon an inner spiritual vitality rather than upon ecclesiastical organization or miraculous claims, and when the basis of its message shifted from the Scriptures and personal religious experience to priestly power and ceremonial efficacy it had nothing in organization or traditional authority upon which it could fall back. So that its sacerdotal development was a weakness both in lessening the contrast to Rome and in removing the fundamental source of its strength. Thus this development helped to bring about the absorption of both the Irish missions and the Irish Church by Rome.

A third cause of the weakening and disappearance of the Irish Christianity was the unnatural monastic ideal which it fostered. The monastic life, which made its way into western Europe in the early part of the fifth century through John Cassian, who founded his monasteries at Marseilles, and Honoratus, whose monastery at Lerins had such widespread influence,[30] was the form in which the Christian ideal was presented to the Irish and through them to those to whom they carried it. In that rough age there was probably an advantage in a community of Christian workers, providing as it did a safe refuge for them and their converts, a place of training for evangelists and missionaries, and a publication house for the Christian Scriptures. Under such conditions, with the added elements of primitive Christian experience and limited knowledge, something might be said for a monastic rule as a guide and help to right living and worth-while Christian service. But when the arguments in favour of the monastic ideal are all in, it remains true that it represents a wholly and fundamentally unnatural life. The exaltation of celibacy, though not given the place by the Irish which it had among the Romans, yet was inevitable in the system, and was an abandonment of the home and the sacredness of the procreative function. The asceticism which the monastic ideal fostered, in spite of the true emphasis which it gave to the supremacy of the things of the spirit, meant a despising of the body as evil and a scorning of the joys of human intercourse as a hindrance to the real objectives of life. And the Irish leaders and missionaries went to the farthest extreme which human ingenuity could devise in a cruel and unnatural austerity. Some of their followers revolted and some succumbed and died, but the ascetic practice held its grip upon the Irish system, with the inevitable

---

[30] See Howorth, *Golden Days of the Early English Church,* i, 169f.

result that when the Benedictine rule was brought in by the Roman missionaries its more human spirit and methods easily made it the victor in the contest.

A fourth cause, really a phase of the monastic cause just mentioned, was the exaltation of the monastery at the expense of the Church. I refer to this elsewhere.[31] So high a place was given to the monastery that all Christian life and the whole organization of that life revolved around the monastery and its abbot, and the churches were quite secondary. This prevented the development of the normal organization of Christian life and activity which is represented by the Church. The mistake of the Irish Christian movement was not, as Anglican writers affirm, in disregarding the bishops and neglecting the unified organization which the episcopal system gave to the Roman communion and later to the Anglican, but in disregarding the basic importance of the Church itself and of its leaders, whether bishops or plain ministers, and in substituting for these the monastery and its autocratic head the abbot. Moreover, as we have seen, Irish monasticism, with an austerity so alien to natural human relationships, ultimately gave way to the Roman system. And when that occurred there was no basis on which the Irish Christianity could rest or in which it could express itself. This neglect of the Church was a fundamental weakness. The Roman leaders were wiser. With them the Church was primary and the monastery secondary.

Thus Irish Christianity disappeared as a distinct movement, due partly to external causes and partly to causes within itself. But its achievements were great during its own lifetime. And through the centuries its influence has continued, with results that are uncounted and in great degree unseen, but which mark it as a permanently effective movement

---

[31] Chapter 3.

in the history of Christianity. It had its weakness, but it
had its strength, and it still makes its contribution to the
world and to us.

III

The Irish missionary movement, as I have just intimated,
is not simply a great fact of the past, unrelated to the present. Like all history, it has significance for our own day,
and meaning for ourselves. Much of what this significance
is has already appeared in what has been said. But it will
be more clear if I sum it up here, bringing together the lessons that have been suggested and perhaps adding others.
First of all, there is the example given to us in the devotion
of these Irish missionaries to Christ and to His missionary
purpose. We have a never-failing resource for encouragement in the missionaries of the past. There is no great name
and no great missionary movement that does not have inspiration for us. But of all the movements and all the
names there is none that has in it more inspiration than the
Irish missionary movement and its outstanding leaders.
These men had a task full large in the home land, but they
heard the call of unevangelized peoples across the water and
went forth with their message. They knew practically
nothing of missionary organization and they could look to
the Christians at home for no support, but they had a trust
in God that gave them a sense of security and made them
certain of success. Travel was very irregular and communication uncertain, and they could hear but seldom from those
they had left behind, but they had resources of encouragement and strength far greater than they could find in human
friendship. It was like sailing uncharted seas for them to set
out on their missionary adventure, so new and so lacking in
precedent, but they had faith in the divine leadership.
Jonas, the biographer of Columbanus, again and again refers

to this. They met difficulties and oppositions and temptations, but never turned back. What Schlunk says of the Moravian missionaries could be said of these early Irish pioneers: " Men hard as steel, with iron will, ready to devote everything to winning one soul to the Saviour." [32]   Call the roll of the leaders, Patrick, Columba, Aidan, Chad, Columbanus, Gall, Fursey, and it seems as though God had sifted the nation to secure the choicest men for His great missionary task—as indeed He had. They were men of rare devotion, in whom Christ had the supreme place and in whose thought His missionary purpose was the dominating idea— " Woe is me if I preach not the gospel." Certainly one lesson we all need all the time, especially as we contemplate our missionary task, is the lesson of faithful devotion to Christ and His world purpose, and in this the Irish missionaries can be our teachers.

The Irish missionary movement has lessons for us also as to the true ideal of the Christian life. I have spoken of the distinctive expression of that ideal on the part of the Irish Christian leaders in the extreme austerity of monasticism, and have compared the Irish and Romans in the place given to the Church as the organized expression of the Christian ideal. The early Irish monasteries apparently started out on a family basis. They were Christian settlements, each family living by itself in a humble cottage, carrying on its life in ordinary fashion, with work in the fields and the home, with family intercourse, and normal friendly social life. Meals were taken in a common central hall, and the church was the centre of the settlement and of its life. Here the Christians cultivated their spiritual life, and were able to protect themselves from pagans who might oppose the followers of the new religion. One is reminded somewhat of John Eliot's

---

[32] *Die Weltmission des Christentums,* 111.

Christian Indian villages. The later monastery, on the other hand, excluded all natural joys and pleasures. Not only was family life left outside, but friendly talk, hearty laughter, and play were strictly taboo, as belonging to the devil. Of course this was in large measure the monastic ideal wherever found, in the Roman Church as in the Irish; only the Irish monks carried it to the furthest extreme. The basis of this ideal was the exaltation of the spirit and the emphasis upon the unseen world and the future life. This is strikingly illustrated by the fact that it is not the birthday of the saints that we note and celebrate, but the deathday—or rather their birthday into the life of the eternal world. After all, here is a fine teaching for us. The great thing is not this world that we see and that is so ever-present with us, but the world unseen yet all around us and that after this present life we shall enter into in a reality and a completeness that we do not know now. The highest things in our life are the things of the spirit, supremely important, with which nothing else is to be compared in value. These are the essential and fundamental aspects of the ideal fostered by the monks. But they added non-essentials. And the lesson for us is to distinguish between the essentials of the Christian ideal and non-essential additions. With all the emphasis of which we are capable we should preach the supreme importance of spiritual things and the spiritual world, but we need to remember also that God has put us in a world of human relationships, a world of beauty and delight, and given us a body and a physical life to use for His glory. A judicious distinction between essentials and non-essentials, with all possible emphasis upon the former and proper use of the latter—this is what we are to learn from the story of the Irish monks.

A third point of significance for us in the Irish missionary movement is the value and importance of education in the missionary enterprise. It is not reading into the record what is not there when we speak of the monasteries of the Irish as monastic *schools*. Nor was it by accident that they became such. It must be remembered that they were centres for the cultivation of the spiritual life, and that the objective source of that life was recognized to be the Bible. On this as a basis the monasteries developed their method and activity. First of all, a thorough understanding of the Scriptures was desired, and that led to exposition of the Word, in which some of the abbots became such outstanding figures. It was this, also, together with the paucity of copies of the Bible, that emphasized the memorizing of large portions of the Psalms and Gospels. For the interpretation of the Scriptures and the enrichment of the spiritual life recourse was also had to more general studies, such as grammar, rhetoric, geometry, Greek and music. Doubtless the eastern origin of the monastic system had something to do with this breadth of cultural interest; though it must be remembered that it was not culture for its own sake, but simply the aid that these cultural studies might give in the interpretation of the Scriptures and the development of personal Christian experience. In other words, the monasteries were never schools in quite the modern sense, but schools in Christian living. However, the point is that they were schools. The significance of this for us in our thought of the missionary enterprise is that when the deep and genuine Christian experience of the young men in the monasteries, and the broad interest represented by their cultural studies and fostered by these studies, stirred the members of the monastic communities to missionary zeal, the monasteries quite naturally became training schools for missions. Thus the Irish missionaries were trained men, well educated, fitted for positions of large leadership, able to establish schools of the prophets like those where they themselves were reared and to train those who should follow in the good succession begun by them. Roman monks, to be sure, were also educated, though—except in England, where the Irish influence was strong and continuing—not so broadly or so thoroughly as the Irish. So notable was the attention given to education among the Irish that at one time in western Europe if a man knew Greek it was almost proof positive that he was an Irishman. Among the distinctive characteristics of the Irish missions none is more notable than the emphasis given to education. That surely is an example for us and a lesson we can most wisely learn and never forget. There is no short cut to knowledge, and goodness and wisdom are not identical. There is no stage in the expanding missionary movement when thorough training of both heart and mind are not needed. Missionaries to primitive peoples need to be well educated quite as much as those going to lands of higher culture. The names of Columba and Aidan and Columbanus illustrate the importance and value of education. They were great missionaries, not only in their personality but in what they were able to achieve. And their achievement was possible largely because of the thoroughness and breadth of their training and education.

I need not mention again the importance of the evangelical message of the Irish missionaries, nor can I here discuss the value of their independence or of the church system which they fostered. What has been said as to the significance of the Irish movement is sufficient to make clear that it is not a movement unrelated to the present, but that it has a rich contribution to make to us in its inspiring personalities, in the permanent forces which were released through it, and in its practical teachings and warnings for missionary policies and ideals in our own day. The more it is studied, the greater will its contribution be found to be.

III

THE MISSIONARY METHODS OF THE MIDDLE
AGES

WE are likely to think of the world of the Middle Ages as though it were a different world from ours. Ten or twelve or fifteen centuries seem a long time. Most of us live entirely in the present. Few of us see our own times against the background of history. Methods of Christian work today may be clear enough, but what have the methods of a thousand years ago to do with our twentieth century methods? That is not so evident. The difficulty is that we do not realize how similar were the conditions of missionary work in the early Middle Ages to those of our own days. To be sure, civilization differed then, and indeed was different in different lands, as is true today. But non-Christian peoples had their own religions, with well-established beliefs and customs of worship; there were religious leaders to be reckoned with; rulers had a close relation to the religious life of the people and hence to the missionaries of a new faith. There was the same reaching after God, the same ability to grasp spiritual ideas, the same preparation in religious life and moral need for the message of Christianity, the same obstacles in human sin, social custom, jealousy or privileged position, political expediency and sectarian division, not to speak of the difficulties of travel, language and adjustment to new conditions. Essentially the conditions of missionary work were similar in the time of Patrick and Columba and Boniface and Otto to those in the

94

time of Ziegenbalg and Carey and Ashmore or the men and women of today. In some lands we are facing new conditions, but in basic things we are not so far from the world of the Middle Ages as we might unthinkingly suppose.

In all ages the question of missionary method is of high importance. How shall the message be presented? What should be the content of the message? Who should be chosen as missionaries? How ought they to be trained? What have the home churches to do with the missionaries and their work? What agencies are to be employed? What shall be the attitude to the faith of the people? What indeed are the aims of missions? These are questions that belong to no one period in the expansion of Christianity, but have to be asked in every age in which our religion is preached. All of these questions are of great importance today: they were as important a thousand or fifteen hundred years ago.

In this practical matter of missionary methods it is quite possible for us to learn from the past. We need all the wisdom and suggestion we can get from any source. We are accustomed to hold innumerable conferences to discover how others do the work, and we try to gather as richly as possible from correspondence and printed literature the ideas and knowledge of other lands and other denominations. That is to say, we are learning wisdom from those who are living and working today. In a similar and not less effective way we may learn from those who have lived and worked in the past, those who have faced similar needs and problems and have worked out their solutions for the times when they lived.

After all, the Gospel is the same in all ages, and human need is the same among all peoples. Fundamental principles are likely to be found permanent, even though methods of applying them may change. It will pay us, then, to study the methods of other days, to see how we may wisely make application of the principles to the needs and conditions of today.

In considering the work of the Middle Age missions the missionaries are of first interest to us. Who were they and how were they appointed? First of all, we notice that they were volunteers. That holds true not only in the early mediæval period, but in the later centuries when the great orders were the agencies of missionary work. Those who entered the orders did so of their free will, and so were volunteers for missionary service. But in a more definite way the missionaries of the earlier centuries were volunteers. They were members of monastic communities or of monastic orders, and were absolutely subject to the will of the superior by their vow of obedience. But so far as foreign service was concerned they seem to have made their own choice. The old Irish life of Columba tells us that after he had sown faith and religion in Ireland and multitudes had been baptized by him and he had organized churches and monasteries, " the determination that he had determined from the beginning of his life came into his mind, namely, to go on a pilgrimage. He then meditated going across the sea to preach the Word of God to the men of Scotland. He went therefore on the journey." Nothing is said as to his being set apart to that mission by a higher authority. We disregard the uncertain tradition of the battle of which he is said to have been the occasion and the consequent advice of his " soul-friend " to devote his life to missionary work. In any case, that was only advice, not authoritative command, and it is clear that he was a volunteer for the foreign work. To be sure, Columba was not then under monastic authority, but was engaged in establishing and conducting his own monasteries. Columbanus, however, his contemporary, was a monk of Bangor, under the headship of the great Comgall, as we have seen. The idea of a foreign mission seems to have come to him quite independently of any suggestion from his abbot, indeed it was present with him from his youth. When he asked permission to go forth as a missionary, Comgall opposed it at first, but only because he thought Columbanus was needed in Ireland. However, when Columbanus pressed the matter the abbot gave his approval. It would seem that the consent of the abbot was necessary, but the choice of the foreign work was wholly a voluntary affair on the part of Columbanus. Aidan's mission to England was suggested to him by the assembly to whom his unsuccessful predecessor reported, and he voluntarily accepted the service. Boniface made choice of the monastic life and studied and served successively at Exeter and Nutescelle until his mind became set upon missionary work abroad, and then apparently of his own free will he sailed with his companions to the Continent; and his appeals for reinforcements were directed to the clergy and others as well as to the abbots and bishops; the numbers who responded were volunteers. Very largely, it would seem,[1] the principle of voluntary enlistment prevailed. It was a great host of volunteers who through the sixth, seventh and eighth centuries streamed forth from their monasteries as foreign missionaries.

As to the call to missionary work, it came in various ways, as in our own day. Patrick was summoned by a vision or dream. " I saw in the night visions," he says, " a man whose name was Victoricus coming as it were from Ireland with countless letters. And he gave me one of them, and I read the beginning of the letter, which was entitled, ' The Voice of the Irish;' and while I was reading aloud the beginning of the letter, I thought that at that very moment I heard the voice of them who lived beside the Wood of Foclut which is nigh unto the western sea. And thus they cried, as with one mouth, ' We beseech thee, holy youth, to come and walk

[1] Augustine, of course, with other missionaries from Rome, were exceptions. They were commissioned by direct papal authority. There was no such dominant authority in England and Ireland.

among us once more.' " [2]   And another night he heard a voice saying, " He Who laid down His life for thee, He it is Who speaketh in thee." Again a third time he dreamed that one was praying as it were within him, " mightily with groanings," and when he awoke he remembered the words of Paul, " The Spirit himself maketh intercession for us with groanings which cannot be uttered." His dreams centred around his experience as a slave in Ireland, and were used by God to call him back to the land of his captivity as a missionary.

Columbanus was called to Christian service through the words of the woman recluse whom he visited as a youth, and his desire for foreign work was stimulated by thinking on the call of God to Abraham, which seemed to be a call to him. Aidan's call came in the recognition by his fellow monks that he himself fulfilled the conditions and possessed the qualifications that he urged were necessary for success in a mission to England. Willibrord heard the call to Christianize the Frisians in the appeal of Egbert, in whose monastery in Ireland he was studying, urging that he take up the work which he himself had desired to undertake but had been prevented from doing. Boniface heard the stories of Willibrord's life and work and was stirred to follow in his footsteps. Thus through the experiences of their lives, through dreams and visions, through the appeals of others, through the stories of missionaries already on the mission field, God called them to the service abroad.

It is instructive to note the qualifications which these missionaries of early days seem to have had. Noteworthy was their zeal for Christ and His work. Columbanus, in the fervour of his devotion, could not be held back even by the wild appeal of his mother in throwing herself across the

---

[2] *Confession*, 23.

threshold of their home to keep him with her. It was not the love of adventure nor the call of romance that stirred the enthusiasm of these missionaries, but a deep and genuine love for God and a feeling like that of Paul when he cried, " Woe is me if I preach not the gospel! " But zeal was not enough; thorough training and education was recognized as necessary. So they spent years of study in monasteries, the universities of that day. Sometimes they entered when scarcely more than boys and stayed until they were grown men, studying and gaining experience. All the outstanding missionaries of those early centuries of whose lives we have full details were men of the most thorough education. A third qualification was experience. They did not undertake the great responsibilities of foreign mission service until they had had years of work at home and had been tested and proved under the careful guidance of wise leaders, perhaps as evangelists, perhaps as teachers, perhaps as priors of monasteries. Their success as missionaries was in most cases assured by success at home. A fourth quality which they possessed was ability for leadership. This, too, they had first proved by experience in the home land. They could each be trusted with responsibility to lead, through ability in organization or administration, or through magnetic personality, or through their tact and wisdom, or through their impressive spirituality and deep piety. There was no missionary society to direct their work and they were thus left almost entirely independent; even those who held official relation to the Roman Church carried on their work with only occasional conference or correspondence with the Pope. So that well-tested powers of leadership were indispensable. The early missionaries had these powers to an outstanding degree.

For the success of these missionaries of the early Middle Ages we must give large credit to the monastic schools where they were trained, and to the great leaders who were their teachers, like Comgall of Bangor, Finnian of Clonard and Finnian of Moville, Columba of Iona, and Germanus of Auxerre. These were men of deep and strong religious experience, with broad and solid learning, and wide outlook and catholic spirit. The Bible held the central place in the curriculum, especially the Gospels and the Psalms, with careful and extended exposition and the committing to memory of large portions. In the Irish monasteries, which, as already noted, were famous centres of learning, Greek was studied, with other general subjects. Very definite and well planned attention was given to the cultivation of the spiritual life. This was not left to the students themselves, nor was it given a subordinate place or made voluntary. Rather was it stressed as the fundamental thing and was carefully organized and directed. Student Volunteers today are urged to observe the " morning watch." But these missionaries throughout their years of training gave many hours of the day, often eight out of the twenty-four, to prayer and meditation and worship. This was quite as thoroughly supervised and as carefully directed as the manual labour or the evangelistic or literary work in which they engaged. They were thoroughly trained for all phases of their great undertaking.

A word may be added as to their relation to the home churches after they had sailed to the foreign field and were at work as missionaries. Most of them, as we have seen, never returned to the home land. Columba was an exception, but his field was only a few hours' sail from Ireland. In almost every case they went with no expectation of ever returning home; though occasional exceptions show that there was no requirement or established custom governing the matter. Facilities or lack of facilities for travel probably constituted the determining factor. The missionaries corresponded with abbots of their home monasteries or with other leaders at home, as opportunity very infrequently presented itself, and such stories and reports of their work as were received were used to inspire the younger men and women—for in some cases women went out as missionaries—and thus some in the home Church were kept in touch with their representatives abroad. Largely in proportion as this latter could be done was the work of the missionaries permanently successful.

Missionaries were expected to secure their own support. So far as we know, they received nothing from the churches or monasteries at home, though occasional gifts by individuals are recorded. Records are relatively meagre, and more regular contributions may have been sent abroad, but the opportunities and facilities for sending them were few and far between. It would seem that some supplies must have been taken by the missionary when he started out, or money for the buying of food, for he had the journey to make and it would be some days before he could make even temporary arrangements for food and shelter. The customary way, as we have seen in the case of Patrick,[3] was to approach first the chief or ruler, present the message to him and win him to the new faith, or at least secure his approval or his consent for Christian missionary work. If the missionary's appeal was successful, he asked for a piece of land on which to build a church or monastery. Here he made his headquarters; and here he and his companions might raise grain and other produce and might keep a few cows and other stock. As the religion of the people was determined by the ruler, it was quite natural for the missionaries to try first to win him to Christ or to induce a favourable attitude toward the Christian faith. After groups of Christians were gathered they would contribute much of what the missionaries needed. But their needs were few. They could sleep in the open air,

---

[3] Chapter 2.

or in a rough shack which they could throw up easily and quickly, and they ate very sparingly and with frequent intervals of fasting. For example, Columbanus directed his fellow-missionaries in the monasteries subject to his rule to eat but two simple meals a day, and these meals were limited to pulse, cabbage, flour mixed with water, and a little portion of biscuit, with fish. Only when guests came was a more elaborate meal indulged in. Some of the missionaries, like Gall, were great fishermen, and this added an enjoyable and cheap dish to their fare; of meat they ate very sparingly. Some of the hagiographies have marvellous stories of the miracles wrought by the missionaries to secure food, as well as to get other things they wanted or needed. But however it came, it was secured by the missionaries themselves in the country where they were at work and was not provided by the churches at home. We have a letter from Boniface to Fuldrad, chaplain of Pepin the Frankish ruler, urging that the king provide means of support for his followers and successors after his death.[4] Columba, on the other hand, had on Iona a regular farm for the support of his community. Of course, it must be remembered that these early mediæval missionaries worked in countries with a temperate climate. Whatever significance their practice of self-support might have for missionary method today would be modified by the fact (among others) that foreign missions are now located mostly in tropical lands, where the climate is very different from that to which the missionaries have previously been accustomed.

How did these missionaries work? What methods did they use in presenting the message? On the one hand, there were wide-ranging preaching tours; on the other, the manifold activities of a central station. The great purpose was evan-

---

[4] *Epis.* lxxix in Migne, lxxxix. col. 779.

gelism—making known the good news and enlisting men and
women as disciples and followers of Christ. This is the key-
note of their message. It appears in abstracts of their
sermons that have come down to us, it conditioned and determined their methods of work. Touring, as I have said,
was one of the chief methods. Usually they travelled in
groups, preaching in villages and towns along the way, and
talking of the things of the kingdom with those whom they
met. Bede says of Aidan that " wherever in the course of
his journeys he saw any, whether rich or poor, he would
there and then invite them, if unbelievers, to embrace the
mystery of the faith, or, if they were believers, he would
strengthen them in the faith and would stir them up by
words and actions to almsgiving and the performance of
good works." [5] Miss Margaret Stokes has told in her interesting account of *Three Months in the Forests of France*
that as one travels along the road in northern France one
comes continually on springs or wells bearing the name of
Fursey, witnessing to his wide travels proclaiming the Gospel. Boniface made long journeys in what is now Saxony,
Hesse-Cassel, Bavaria and other parts of Germany, as well
as in Holland, where he finished his life as a martyr. Sometimes the missionary had to use an interpreter, but the most
successful spoke in the vernacular of the people. Patrick,
of course, knew the Irish tongue from his years of captivity
in that land. Columba worked principally among those who
were of his own race and language, but needed an interpreter
when he went to the Picts. Columbanus may have used an
interpreter at times, though many if not most of those to
whom he preached, in Burgundy at least, would understand
Latin, which was familiar to him. Gall was a famous linguist and " had not a little knowledge not only of Latin but

---

[5] *Hist. Eccles.*, iii, 5.

also of the barbarian language." [6] Boniface learned or knew the language of the Germans. The means of transportation which the missionaries used were usually their own stout legs, though other facilities were used when available or necessary, like the " chariot " or cart used by Patrick or the boats on which Columba had to travel among the islands or on the lochs and rivers.

A second phase of the method employed by these pioneer missionaries is that which centres around the monastery. This was the central station, from which the activities of the mission extended into the surrounding country, and from which the missionaries and their associates went out on the tours of evangelization. The first thing that Columba did on his arrival in Iona was to establish a monastery—just a small group of rude buildings, a central oratory for worship, a few huts for shelter, some outbuildings for the grain and cattle. Columbanus built three monastic institutions at Luxeuil, Annegray and Fontaine, which became famous throughout the land and to which multitudes flocked. Boniface founded Fulda and many other monastic centres for men and women. The use of the monastery as the agency for missionary work was the accepted method and practice.

Within the monastery there was a wide variety of activities. Some of the monks attended to the household duties, in the kitchen or elsewhere. Some worked in the fields or cared for the stock. Others more advanced, who were well trained for the work, gave themselves through long hours to making copies of the Bible or of parts of it, or providing catechisms or service books. Special attention was given to this literary work in the Irish monasteries, where, as has been noted, education held a high place. A large portion of each day was given to worship and prayer, stated hours

[6] Robinson, *Conversion of Europe*, 314n.

being observed in the chapel and much time being spent in private devotions. The older monks, or those who were most experienced or best qualified, had the responsibility of leading the worship of the community. The Benedictine monasteries gave particular attention to industries and art, hardly any form of these being neglected, with the result that in many cases a community or village grew up, in which the monastery was not only the religious centre but also the centre of culture and learning. The influence of the monastery, and of the Christian missionaries who made it their headquarters, was much extended by the founding of branches of the chief monastery. This was quite a common custom, as we find in the stories of Columba, Columbanus and others.

An important element in the method of the missionaries of the earlier mediæval period, especially those of the Irish churches, was the attention to the Bible which has already been mentioned. The Roman missionaries apparently laid more stress upon liturgy and the forms of worship. Augustine, writing to the Pope a year after his arrival in England, makes inquiry about a good many details of liturgy. Gradually the Irish gave increased emphasis to liturgical forms and practices, but in the earlier days the Bible was used as the chief instrument in winning the people to Christianity. Patrick's writings are saturated with Scripture. Columba is said by Adamnan, his biographer, to have used the Word of God as the great instrument in conversion. Columbanus wrote commentaries on the Psalms. The wonderful decoration or illumination of the copies of the Bible made in the monasteries of Ireland, Scotland and England show the place which the Scriptures had in the thought and plans of the Irish leaders. The relation which the Roman missionaries had with the ecclesiastical organization explains the greater emphasis which they placed upon liturgy and the forms of the Church. Both Bible and liturgy were in Latin, which was recognized as the ecclesiastical language. Of course this needed translation by the missionary when it was read to the people, but this was not so great a handicap as it would have been had copies of the Bible been common and the people been able to read it. Few could read, and books of any kind were scarce. But the missionaries were well instructed, and they could use the Latin freely and could translate and explain in the tongue of the people.

Mention has been made of the place that was given to the cultivation of the spiritual life in the education and work of the monks. One needs only to read the lives of the saints or such writings as have come down from their hands to appreciate the emphasis which was laid upon the devotional life. Patrick's *Confession* breathes the spirit of devotion, and his *Lorica* is really a prayer. The writings of Columbanus are full of the same spirit and his monastic rule gives detailed directions for prayer and devotion. Columba's intercessory prayer for his associates as they worked in the field, to which reference is made elsewhere,[7] is a good illustration of his own practice. Boniface laid very great stress on intercessory prayer, and gave careful attention to the enlisting of intercessors both in Germany and in England. He wrote to Egbert, Archbishop of York, "With heartfelt prayers we entreat your clemency, that your piety would pray for us in our labours and dangers, for great necessity presses upon us to seek the help of the just, as it is written, ' The persistent prayer of a just man availeth much.' "[8] He wrote to others in the same strain. And in his monasteries he organized intercessory prayer on a systematic basis, the Fraternity Book of the monastery listing the names of those for whom regular prayer was made by the monks. Other examples might be given of this emphasis upon intercessory prayer.

---

[7] See Chapter 2.
[8] *Epis.* xxxviii, quoted by Robinson, *op. cit.*, 379.

Something more should be said about the relation of these early missionaries to the government. I have pointed out that it was the common practice to try first, on coming into a new field of effort, to gain the favour and approval of the chief or king. This friendly alliance between the religious and the secular powers was quite the rule, but the religious leaders maintained their independence and refused to allow the secular authorities to limit them or their work in any way. On the other hand, they made use of the rulers to aid in their missionary work, as occasion offered. Oswald, king of Northumbria, worked hand in hand with Aidan, and was almost as powerful a factor in the evangelization of northern England as the great missionary himself. Boniface freely used the active help of Charles Martel, saying that without his patronage he could neither rule the people nor defend the priests or deacons, the monks or nuns, nor without his mandate and the awe which he inspired could he put a stop to the rites of the pagans and the sacrileges of idol-worship.[9] This borders closely upon compulsion by the secular authority, but Boniface probably did not seek more than the strong influence of the government, so far as positive effort in making Christians was concerned. It was only the moral influence of Ethelbert, king of Kent, that Augustine used, for Bede says of those who came in numbers to hear the Christian preaching, " Their conversion he is said to have encouraged, but only so far that he compelled no one to embrace Christianity, but only embraced with a closer affection those who believed in being heirs with himself of the heavenly kingdom. For he had learned from his instructors and those who were the instruments of his salvation that the service of Christ ought to be voluntary and not compulsory." [10] In later times the attitude of the Roman mission-

---

[9] *Epis.* xii, quoted by Robinson, *op. cit.*, 361.
[10] *Hist. Eccles.*, i, 26.

aries radically changed, and they not only did little or nothing to keep enthusiastic monarchs like Charlemagne from adding to political efforts a Christianizing by the sword, but in some cases—Otto in the twelfth century is an example—definitely used the power of the civil authority to compel acceptance of the Christian faith. It was inevitable that alliance with secular authority should run into this excess; the danger was not foreseen in the early years.

I

We have looked at the missionary in these early days, and have seen how he was called to the work, how he was trained, and what his relation was to the churches which he left at home. We have seen him at his work, and have watched him in his missionary tours and in his central monastery. We have observed him making large use of the Bible or liturgy, always emphasizing the devotional life and the practical use of prayer. And we have seen how increasingly he worked in co-operation with the secular authority. Now let us consider the Church, as the missionaries built it in the new lands where they proclaimed the Christian faith.

The Church held a very different place on the one hand among the Irish and on the other hand among the Romans. In the early days of Irish Christianity there were no monasteries, though there were Christian communities, " clans re-organized under a religious form," [11] where whole families lived and sought to nurture their spiritual life. Those established by Patrick seem to have been of this character. It was not the monastery but the Church that received chief emphasis and held the principal place. Patrick and his followers founded churches wherever they made converts, and before Patrick's death these were to be found almost all over

---

[11] Montalembert, *The Monks of the West,* iii, 86.

Ireland. It was natural that these churches should look to him as their leader, and quite as natural that he should bring them into a united organization under himself, in accordance with custom prevailing widely in the Christian Church. While there were other bishops, he was supreme, with his episcopal headquarters at Armagh. Probably he thought of himself and his churches as part of the great Christian fellowship, and like most of the Christians of the West held the bishop of the Church at Rome in high honour. But there is no satisfactory historical evidence that he ever had any formal or official relation to the Pope, or ever thought of the churches as part of the Roman organization. In his earlier life he purposed to visit the Pope, as the outstanding Christian leader in the West, but it is practically certain that he never actually went to Rome. With Patrick, then, the local church was the regular and natural Christian organization, and in accordance with the common practice he grouped these churches into a national organization.

When the religious life in Ireland had declined, in the century following Patrick's death, it was revived through the agency of the monasteries. These were introduced from Britain, through Finnian and others, as already described. Monasticism was at this time spreading through all the Christian world, West as well as East, and the monastic life was coming to be thought of universally as presenting the ideal for the Christian. As centres of spiritual culture and as agencies for the spread of Christianity the monasteries provided an organization which did for that day what in the earlier years had been done more informally and less systematically by the churches. The Roman Church, with its developing authority and imperialism, took the monastic movement under its aegis, guided it, and kept the Church in the ascendancy. The Irish churches, however, having a looser and only a national or even tribal organization, yielded their place of eminence to the monasteries. The result was that in the two centuries and more after Patrick the monastery was the chief organization and the Church occupied quite a secondary place. Some of the monasteries, Columba's, for example, were ruled by prebyters, that is, ordained ministers, and had among the monks under their direction one or more bishops. This was a unique situation, not found outside of the Celtic system. So far as the ordinary life and work of the monastery was concerned the bishop was quite subordinate to the abbot, and only took the leading position when there was ordaining or similar episcopal duties to be performed. This is sufficient indication of the different attitude which had come to be assumed toward the Church. Churches were subordinate parts of the monastic organization and were subject to the abbot. But the work of the Church went on, preaching was regularly done, the ordinances were performed, personal spiritual needs were cared for. The difference was that the monasteries, with their abbots and priors, were dominant, and not the churches, with their bishops and other clerical leaders.

The Roman missionaries, too, were monks, as were the Irish. But, as I have said, the Church took the monasteries and the orders into its organization and directly or indirectly controlled their work. Thus the Church retained its leading position. Bishops and archbishops were ordained, synods were held, missionaries made occasional or frequent visits to Rome, and the relation of the churches founded by the missionaries to the ecclesiastical authority centreing in Rome and the Pope was constantly emphasized and strengthened. The rapidly developing imperial outreach and centralized authority enabled the Roman Church to make itself the chief Christian organization; but it was the general body, the Church as it centred in Rome, that was emphasized, not the local churches.

The church buildings erected by the Irish missionaries were simple and plain. In the monastery the oratory occupied the central position, surrounded by the common hall and the huts of the monks. But the oratory was a small structure, with one room and no apse; so with all their church buildings. The Saxon Church, which was typical of early churches of Roman faith, added the apse, and rapidly developed the form and decoration of later times. The Irish service and organization were simple, while the Roman tended increasingly to elaborateness, and this difference is manifested in the form of the church buildings. In other words, the church buildings represented the Christian message and ideal as interpreted and taught by these two different Christian groups.

In the development of the Church a practical question arose as to the attitude which should be taken towards the non-Christian customs. Those which were directly related to pagan worship were of course opposed with utmost sternness and unyielding insistence. Worship of Thor and Odin, or of the sun, was directly the opposite of the worship of the one Creator, and of His Son Jesus Christ. One or the other must be chosen; there could be no compromise. So with magic and offerings to gods and spirits. The rejection of Columbanus by the Alemanni of Switzerland was due to his strenuous opposition to the idolatrous customs of the people. At Bregenz, where he and Gall made their headquarters in an ancient Christian church, they found three idols on the walls, which the people said were the gods which protected them. Gall urged them to give up their idolatry, but Columbanus seized the images and broke them in pieces, throwing them into the lake near by. Dr. van Dyke's story, *The First Christmas Tree,* gives a pretty accurate view of the attitude and custom of Boniface (Winfried). No quarter was given to the things of pagan worship.

On the other hand, customs which were not distinctively
religious were generally not opposed. Of course there was a
racial similarity between the Britons and the Irish, between
the Scots of Ireland and those of Scotland, between the Celts
of Ireland and of Gaul, between the Saxons and the Germans, which meant little difference in popular customs, except as these were connected with religious practices. So
these customs were likely to be understood by the missionaries and there was not much ground for opposition. The
missionaries were not greatly concerned with changing the
culture or civilization of the people to whom they went, but
laid their major emphasis, almost their exclusive emphasis,
upon the religious message, the worship of the true God and
salvation through Christ His Son.

But there were pagan customs which might be sublimated
and used. A Christian meaning might be put into them, so
that they could be retained and be given a place in Christian
life and worship. At least some thought so and suited their
practice to their thought. O'Donovan, in his edition of the
Annals of the Four Masters,[12] says that " Patrick engrafted
Christianity on the pagan superstitions with so much skill
that he won the people over to the Christian religion before
they understood the exact difference between the two systems of belief." But while this may suggest a rather more
superficial work than seems to be the fact, there is evidence
that Patrick did use the pagan beliefs in explaining his message and in establishing its practice. The attitude of the
Roman missionaries in England was determined by Pope
Gregory, whose interesting letter to Mellitus, one of Augustine's companions and first Bishop of London, later Archbishop of Canterbury, is preserved by Bede.[13] He directed
that the heathen temples should not be destroyed, but only

---

[12] P. 131n.   [13] *Hist. Eccles.*, i, 30.

the idols in them. Holy water should be sprinkled in the temples, altars installed, and relics placed there. To take the place of the heathen festivals with their sacrifices of oxen, the anniversaries of the death of the martyrs whose relics were preserved were to be observed, huts of boughs being erected around the churches, and oxen being slaughtered for the feast. An important question is raised by the explanation which he gives of his attitude: " For there is no doubt that it is impossible to efface everything at once from their obdurate minds, for the man who strives to ascend to the highest place rises by degrees or steps and not by leaps." The practice of Boniface seems to have been governed by much the same spirit as that indicated by Gregory. In estimating this attitude of both Irish and Roman missionaries, one must recognize that they very generally believed in magical powers and miraculous acts that seem to us only superstitions—though it is possible that the biographers of the saints in later centuries were more credulous than the saints themselves. The missionaries were not different, however, from the people generally in their time. And what seemed important religiously to the Christian missionaries or the pagans might have very little meaning with us. Whatever significance there is in the attitude of the missionaries lies in the principles which they followed, not the details of their practice.

If the churches which the missionaries established were to be permanent they must be provided with leaders. So the question what the missionaries did to secure such leaders becomes important. We are especially interested in the question in view of the modern emphasis on the development of native leaders. We notice first of all that evangelization was carried on by the most available agency, whether that were native or foreign. The missionaries recognized themselves as foreigners—Columbanus, for example, felt this in his relations with the Gallican bishops—but so far as possible identified themselves with their adopted country and made no distinction between the nationals of the land and workers from their home land. As late as the year 748, or thereabouts, thirty years after he had begun his work in Germany, Boniface received a large group of reinforcements from England in response to his appeal for help. These seem to have been placed in positions of responsibility because of the disappointingly slow development of the German converts. Patrick, Columba and Columbanus made large use of foreign workers who had accompanied them or who came to their aid from the home land. For a time, longer in some cases and shorter in others, both foreign missionaries and native workers laboured together, taking such places of responsibility as they were fitted to assume.

But gradually native workers took the place of the foreigners. Within a half dozen decades after Patrick's death the Christian leaders of Ireland were of Irish birth. Columbanus took twelve Irish companions with him on his missionary expedition to France, and added others from Brittany, but when he was expelled from Burgundy only these were allowed or compelled to accompany him, and a considerable number of Gallic associates remained behind, many of whom became important leaders in the work. Jonas, who wrote the life of Columbanus a quarter of a century after his death, and was a monk of Bobbio, Columbanus' Italian monastery, was a native of Italy. The change to native leadership took place gradually, as those born in the land became trained and fitted for larger tasks. Nationalistic self-consciousness had not arisen to make unjustifiable demands, nor did the foreign missionaries hesitate to put in their own places nationals of the country where they were working, like Eustace, for example, the successor of Columbanus at Luxeuil.

But much attention was given to the training of these

native leaders, quite as much as to that of the missionaries themselves. A striking illustration of the care taken by the Irish missionaries to secure worthy successors appears in the case of Aidan, who selected promising Anglo-Saxon boys, twelve at first, more later, whom he trained for the work of leadership in the Church. Among these, as we have seen, was Chad, or Ceadda, who became Bishop of York, and his brother Cedd, later Bishop of the East Saxons. Eata, a successor of Aidan at Lindisfarne, was another. The monasteries which the Irish missionaries established provided excellent facilities for this training. Here they lived in company with their missionary leader, here they studied the Bible and the related subjects which were thought helpful for the work, from these as centres they went out on tours of evangelization under the direction of the abbot, and thus through many years of training and experience they received the preparation which made them worthy successors of the great pioneers. So that the later leaders were nationals, trained under the immediate direction of the missionaries, and thoroughly fitted to build up a Church which should be on the one hand independent and indigenous and on the other related to Christians across the sea, a part of the Christian fellowship in many lands.

II

What is the meaning of all this to our day? Can we learn anything for the work of Christian missions today from the methods used by these pioneers of a thousand years ago? First, as to the type of missionary. One is impressed, in a study of these early missionaries, with the emphasis which was laid upon their spiritual qualifications. They had thoroughly proved themselves in this. The devotional life had become natural for them, and they had given full evidence of their consecration to Christ and His service. This must still and always be the primary and principal qualification. In these days, when many of the people of the land to which the missionaries go have as good education or culture as the missionaries themselves, it is of even more importance than formerly that the foreign leaders should be men and women who have seen the King and who live constantly in His presence. It is only great Christians who make great missionaries, and we cannot substitute high training or outstanding skill for proved Christian character. Perhaps we need to pay more attention to this than in many cases we are doing. But that does not mean that we can neglect thorough training, in education and experience. These early missionaries spent many years in the best schools in the world in preparation for their life task, and we make no mistake in urging and requiring full scholastic training. Unfortunately, mission boards still allow the pressure of immediate need to overbalance the importance of full training, and send men and women to the work with shortened courses of study or without the years of experience which every missionary needs. Notably in the home mission field is the standard lower than it should be. In both home and foreign work additional years of study on the part of the prospective missionary, and closer observation of his service in the home churches on the part of the board, is a pressing necessity. The missionary chooses his work as a life task: we may well stress this still. And for the great task the best is still not too good.

In the missionary's work itself the points of emphasis are significant. First of all, with these missionaries of the Middle Ages evangelism had the chief place. Of course we must recognize that those were not the days of books and widespread education, and the emphasis which we are putting upon school work was not to be expected. But, on the other hand, the Irish missionaries, and to a large extent the Ro-

man, were trained in the best schools to be found and were
men of wide and thorough learning. They gave those who
were to be leaders of the churches the best education possible, but they did not themselves very generally engage in
teaching in the community. They gave themselves with
strenuous devotion to the work of evangelism. With the
differing conditions of today doubtless the proportion of
emphasis may properly be different. But it is possible that
we have gone to an extreme and need to re-examine the place
and purpose of our educational work. Certainly evangelism
must still be the chief thing. In most mission fields it does
not hold the pre-eminent place which it once had. But
nothing can take its place. We can learn a needed lesson in
this from these missionaries of a past day.

Evangelism did not mean simply wide touring. The policy
of concentration was followed. The monastery was the centre from which all the work reached out. And when new
fields were developed there were new monasteries established
as new centres for the expanding work. The policy of concentration is the approved policy for today. But expansion
must go with it, or the missionary zeal of both the missionary
and the Church will be dulled.

Two other points may be mentioned. One is the place
occupied by the Bible and prayer. We may be encouraged in
all our efforts for Bible translation, Bible publishing, and
Bible teaching by the emphasis the early missionaries laid
upon the Book of books. It must always be the centre of the
missionary's study and the centre of all his work. Undoubtedly the larger place which prayer occupied in their programme was wiser than the smaller place which we accord to
it. Activity is the chief thing with us. We are too crowded
to give unhurried time to prayer, in adequate spiritual culture for ourselves or in the intercession which the work and
workers need. Less should be demanded of our missionaries,

and it should be definitely set before them that they are expected to do this larger thing that prayer means. Of course, in the last analysis, the matter rests with the individual missionary, but the boards are not free from responsibility. Definite plans for their service in prayer may be suggested, and clear expectation as to this phase of their work may be definitely and frequently set before them, while equal stress is laid upon this vital feature in the programme of home Church cultivation. The other point is the relation of the missionary to the government. It is evident that official connection with the government led to unevangelical and unchristian methods of work. It is evident, also, that lasting good results were secured only when the mission maintained its independence of the government or its supremacy over it. When the government could control the mission in anything the mission lost its effectiveness. We must not forget the lesson. Its relation to the present situation is too large to be considered here. But it may be well to study again the experience of these early missionaries in view of pressing conditions on the mission field today.

What of the Church? One lesson that stands out is the fact that the Church is essential for the permanence of Christianity wherever it is preached. Undoubtedly the Irish leaders who built their work around the monastery, to the subordinating of the churches as such, were not as wise as the Roman missionaries who exalted the Church. Of course, this is not to say that the latter were wise in their overemphasis on ecclesiastical organization and the subordinating of the local churches to the hierarchy and Rome. But always it has been true that the Church is the agency for permanency in the proclamation of the Gospel and the development of the Christian life. May this not have some bearing upon the tendency seen in some countries to substitute " Christianizing " for " proselytizing " (to use the antithesis sometimes heard), urging the acceptance of Christian belief and the practice of Christian ethics without definite enlistment in the Christian Church?

Our modern emphasis on the training of leaders is not modern, after all, for the missionaries of long ago emphasized the same thing. They did it thoroughly, and we can do no less. But native leadership was not the chief thing; a national Church was not the highest ideal. The dangers in the present nationalistic movement among Christians in mission lands are evident, in the narrowing of Christian fellowship and the dulling of the missionary spirit. The movement has immense advantages in the development of self-consciousness and initiative, but it does not represent the highest ideal or objective, which is Christian fellowship in its widest international reach, and the carrying of the Gospel to unevangelized peoples, even before the fullest self-development is attained at home. Above all, there must be no compromise with non-Christian faiths, however much they may represent the national culture. Christianity still has a message that sets it apart and above all other faiths and lifts it above national cultures and national organizations of religious life. The most important thing for us today is the discovering of the essential character of that message and the best and truest methods by which it can be made known and made dominant. In such a study the missions of the early mediæval centuries hold possibilities of large contribution and help.

IV

THE DEVELOPMENT OF THE MISSIONARY IDEA
IN PROTESTANTISM

PROTESTANTISM was not born with the missionary idea full-grown. It was a hundred and fifty years after Luther nailed his theses on the door of the cathedral church at Wittenberg, before von Weltz sent forth his full-toned missionary call, and nearly two hundred years before a Protestant foreign mission was established. The idea developed slowly, and is still developing.

Missions were in full swing in the Roman Catholic Church in 1517. The friars of the Franciscan and Dominican orders, with the Augustinians of earlier date, were at work in America and Africa and Asiatic lands, and the Jesuits began in the middle of the sixteenth century their almost unexampled missionary endeavours. By the middle of the seventeenth century Roman Catholic missions were to be found in India and China and the Philippines, in west and east Africa, in South and Central America, while even a century later the only missionary work being carried on by Protestants, apart from that among the Indians in the English colonies of the Atlantic seaboard, and the meagre missions of the Dutch East India Company, was the small Danish mission in southeast India and the scattered missions of the Moravians. Through centuries the missionary idea in the Roman Church had developed with the developing Church, and it was part and parcel of the plan and purpose of the Church. In fact, it was missions that had made the Church what it was. The imperial idea, that had made it into the world-reaching organization which it had become, was simply the missionary idea. And missions were accepted as a matter of course— the natural method in the Church's activity and the natural expression of its life. So that the missions of the Roman Church were spread widely over the world and its missionaries were at work among the peoples of every continent.

On the other hand, as has been said, for nearly two centuries Protestants undertook no missionary work, except that among the American Indians. This was important, but it was very small and quite local, and did not grip any large section of the Protestant Church. Occasional voices were to be heard calling for the undertaking of missionary activity, and here and there were individuals who set out by themselves to carry the Gospel to the heathen; there were also a few futile politico-missionary schemes. These last had no solid religious basis, and the individual efforts had no organized support; all were temporary and had no future. The important point to be noted is that the Church of Protestantism was not committed to the missionary undertaking. No group of Protestants was prepared to carry on missionary work; for no group had grasped the missionary idea. The significance of this is not to be seen in 1517, but rather in the decades that followed that date. Through all the early Reformation period there was no missionary enterprise. As Mirbt significantly puts it, " One can write a history of the Reformation without using the word missions." [1]

But more important than the lack of missionary activity was the lack of the missionary idea. That is what makes Mirbt's remark so significant. Circumstances might make it temporarily impossible for Protestants to undertake missionary endeavour. Some of those circumstances were perhaps

---

[1] Mirbt, C., *Missions und Reformation*, 4.

in evidence. But we look in vain for an expression of regret
that they were prevented from beginning the enterprise, or
of hope and longing for the time when the way would open
for missionary outreach. The discoveries that were giving to
Europe a new world were seen by the Roman Church as the
signal for a great missionary advance; but they appeared to
mean nothing to Protestants. As Warneck says, " We miss
in the reformers not only missionary action, but even the
idea of missions, in the sense in which we understand them
today." [2] There were ample difficulties—we shall note them
shortly—but not more than the first century Church faced
when it sent out the great apostle and his associates to con-
quer the world for Christ, or even the Church of the early
Middle Ages when it set out to evangelize Asia and the continent of Europe. Had the missionary idea gripped the
hearts of Protestants as it later gripped the Moravians, or
Carey, or large numbers of Christians in our day, nothing
could have kept them back from the effort to carry to every
land the evangelical message and experience that had so
revolutionized their life; at the very least there would have
been lamentations over the necessity of delay in the undertaking. But of such effort or such regret we hear nothing.
They did not read rightly the New Testament message, they
did not see the vital connection between one's personal experience of Christ and the necessity of making Him known
to all men. The missionary idea was inherent in Christianity,
and above all in evangelical Christianity, but it had yet to be
grasped and understood, it had yet to be developed.

I

We shall see the situation more clearly if we look into the
attitude of the chief Reformation leaders. Luther frequently

---

[2] Warneck, G., *Outline of a History of Protestant Missions*, 9.

speaks of the heathen, and of the necessity of sending preachers to them to declare to them the Word of God, but he uses " heathen " (die Heiden) in the common German meaning of Gentiles, either non-Jewish or non-Christian.[3] He nowhere calls for missionaries to go to the non-Christian world as we know it. Luther looked for the spread of the Gospel over the earth, but not through missionaries, rather through captives and travellers and similar means. The Christian movement had been given its universal aspect by the apostles, and so it had been already preached to all the nations. Moreover, Luther expected the early end of the age—" The end is at hand, at the very threshold "—" The world will perish shortly "—and there was not time for wide preaching of the Gospel, which indeed he believed to have been offered to all already. The heathen world as we understand it was not in Luther's view, and the missionary idea was quite absent from his mind and purpose.

Luther assumed that missions, carried on definitely and systematically, were a work belonging to the apostles.[4] Melanchthon took the same position and supported it by dogmatic argument. In fact, according to his view, the voice of the Gospel had been sounding forth since the time of Adam, and especially through Christians who have been living or travelling in various parts of the world. " Everywhere there are some who teach truly, in Asia, Cyprus, Constantinople. God marvellously stimulates the voice of the Gospel, that it may be heard by the whole human race." So that there is no need for missions or missionaries. The missionary idea was not in Melanchthon's mind. He does not so much argue against missions as he assumes the spread of Christianity through means that make missions unnecessary.

---

[3] Warneck, *op. cit.*, 10.
[4] On the whole question of the attitude of the reformers see Warneck, *Outline of History of Protestant Missions*, 10 f.

Zwingli came a little nearer to an acceptance of the idea of missionary endeavour. The apostles, he affirmed, had carried the Gospel into most parts of the earth, but there still remain very many to be won. But this must be done by apostles, evidently meaning those who are definitely called and set apart by God for that purpose. The Church has nothing to do with the matter: it belonged to the apostles in the beginning, it belongs to apostles now.

Calvin, in his exposition of the Great Commission, deals with it simply in its relation to the apostles. He taught that the Gospel and Christ's kingdom are not to be advanced by the work of men, but that this is the work of God alone. This, of course, would not encourage the undertaking of missions by the Church. In accordance with his own practice he held that rulers had a special duty to spread Christianity in their lands—a phase of the doctrine of *cujus regio ejus religio* that figured so prominently later. Calvin's theological attitude effectively kept him from seeing the missionary duty that is involved in Christian discipleship.

Beza, in his reply to Saravia,[5] insisted that in the Great Commission one must distinguish between what refers to the apostles and what belongs to all Christians: the apostles were sent out to all nations, all Christians are always to preach the Gospel. While the Church is to extend the kingdom, Beza has only vague ideas as to its missionary duty. The missionary idea did not grip him.

Gerhard also opposed Saravia with dogmatic arguments. He insisted that the Gospel had been preached to all men three times: through Adam, through Noah, and through the apostles. He presented an extraordinary proof that the Gospel had been proclaimed to all nations, by summoning the peoples of all the continents and showing evidence that the

---

[5] See *infra*.

message had long ago been given to them. But what evidence! America had received the Gospel long ago, for did not Paul say that the Gospel had brought forth fruit in the whole world? Mexicans had received it, probably from the Ethiopians, because both peoples connected baptism and circumcision. In Peru there was a belief in immortality and a flood, in India the people were acquainted with incarnations, in China a picture had been discovered with three heads looking toward one another—quite evidently referring to the Trinity. So as to other peoples—all clearly proving that the Gospel had been preached already to all nations, as commanded in the Great Commission. At any rate, according to Gerhard, the command to preach in the whole world belonged solely to the apostles: " The command to preach the Gospel in the whole world ceases with the apostles." If Gerhard had had the missionary idea he would have quite argued it out of himself by such reasoning.

The theological faculty of the University of Wittenberg added its argument against missions in a formidable " opinion " on the Great Commission, in which they stated that the command to go into all the world was a personal privilege of the apostles, like gifts of miracles, and had already been fulfilled: that as the Gospel had been preached to all peoples through Adam, Noah and the apostles it was their own fault if they did not now have it; and that it was now the duty of rulers to see to the preaching of the Word, " so that everywhere the true knowledge of God shall be spread." Not a word as to the duty and privilege of missions on the part of the Church.

It is evident, then, that the leaders of Protestantism in the early days had no conception of missions as an essential of Christianity, and as a duty inherently belonging to Christians and the Christian Church. And ordinary members of the churches would not be likely to go farther than their leaders. Roman Catholics brought up this lack of missionary teaching and activity as a charge against Protestantism, for they saw clearly that missions belong by nature to the Gospel. But Protestants had not grasped the missionary idea.

There were reasons for this situation. Probably the most important was the fact that in the beginning and for many decades Protestants were occupied with establishing and maintaining their position. The Roman Church was summoning all its forces of authority and argument to crush the rising evangelical movement, and the empire threw all its powers back of the efforts of the Church. Everywhere there was preaching to be done by the reformers on the theme of justification by faith, there were arguments to be written and answers made to ecclesiastical and civil authorities, there were commentaries to be prepared and hymns to be composed, there were princes and religious leaders to be won to the side of the new movement. All this and more had to be done by a few, and for the larger work of missions there appeared as yet no time. But there was time for what seemed to be important; missions were not conceived as important.

Next in significance was the fact that mission lands were mostly in the hands of Roman Catholic authorities. The newly-discovered territories in South America were controlled by Spain and Portugal. The same was true of most of India and the East Indies. The fate of a Protestant mission in those countries might be imagined from the experience of the Huguenot colony in Brazil, quickly wiped out by the Roman Catholic Portuguese. Protestant lands for a long time were not in touch with mission fields in either West or East. Particularly was this true of Germany, the home of the Reformation, which was not a colonizing country. The lack of available mission fields was enough, it might seem, to discourage any attempt to arouse the Church to missionary interest and effort. But no serious attempt was made to break through the closed circle and to find a mission field.

A third reason was the identification of Protestantism with nationalism. The Protestant movement was furthered by the effort of German rulers to establish their independence of the empire. Luther and other leaders sought the support of these princes and other rulers, partly to win them personally to the evangelical faith, partly to offset the power of the Roman Catholic empire, partly because they believed it was the duty of rulers to care for the religion of their subjects (*cujus regio ejus religio*). The movement for nationalism went hand in hand with the Reformation movement. The imperial idea was narrowed to that of the nation. Nationalism is never favourable to the missionary concept, and this stood in the way of the development of the missionary idea on the part of the leaders of the Reformation.

A fourth reason, somewhat related to the reason just mentioned, was the emphasis which Protestantism laid upon individual interest as opposed to social. It was the faith of the individual which was stressed, and his resulting personal justification. As one has said, " Much emphasis was laid upon grace, but little upon the duty of following Christ in service." The interest was theological rather than practical, individual rather than social. So it was that even Luther opposed with utmost vehemence the peasants' uprising, and apparently saw no justice in their demands. The missionary instinct in the Protestant evangel would some day broaden Christian interest to the widest social ministry, but with the reformers the centre of interest was the individual's relation to God. That effectively prevented the expansion of their thought to a missionary outreach.

Other reasons have already been mentioned: the theological attitude, as in the case of Calvin; the expectation of the early ending of the present age, as with Luther; the misinterpretation of the Great Commission, which grew in absurdity with the development of anti-mission arguments. But none of these reasons, nor all of them together, could be sufficient to excuse the lack of interest in the missionary expansion of the Christian faith. As already pointed out, the difficulties were not greater in Reformation times than they were in apostolic days, or even in the early Middle Ages. They were different, but not greater. The real, essential reason for the absence of missions from the programme of the Reformation leaders was their failure to grasp the missionary idea itself. It was not in their thought or their interpretation of Christianity. Schlunk points this out, saying that " so essential a part of Christianity as missions cannot be lost again after it once has been recognized as necessary on principle." [6] The fact is, it had not been recognized as necessary; the missionary idea as an essential element in Christianity had not been grasped at all.

Yet Protestantism was essentially missionary. It had in it the germs which would inevitably develop into a missionary enterprise. The personal experience of God's saving grace, which was the central idea in the new message, must surely mean the sharing of that experience with others, discontent and unrest until everyone has that experience. That sharing became a reality when the uppermost thing came to be the experience itself rather than the doctrine. Growing out of this central idea of individual justification was the idea of freedom. Even in the early days that idea expressed itself, in the fact of the varying interpretations of doctrine and church organization as represented by Luther, Zwingli, Calvin, Hübmaier and other names. There was to be no central authority in Protestantism as in the Roman Church, which would decide what the message was and how it was to be proclaimed and where. Protestant groups everywhere would assume the freedom to carry the Gospel wherever they

---

[6] Schlunk, Martin, *Die Weltmission des Christentums*, 85.

wished, however different their views might be from those prevailing. That presents to all in the Protestant fellowship the widest opportunity and the fullest encouragement for missionary endeavour. And a third idea, related to those mentioned, was the establishment of independent, self-sufficient churches among those to whom the message was carried, churches which would themselves become centres of extension in missionary service in proportion as the central idea of personal experience of God's grace became a reality in them. Protestantism, therefore, had basically a missionary urge within it, vital not formal, resting back in the heart of the message and the experience of those who accepted in themselves that message, and not at all dependent upon ecclesiastical or political ambitions or aims. The early Protestant leaders did not sense this idea. But sooner or later it would take hold. How it did so I will undertake to show.

II

The seventeenth century marked the real beginning of the expression of the missionary idea. In New England missionary work was in some measure carried on from the earliest times. The charter which authorized the establishment of the Plymouth colony by the Pilgrims expressed the aim that " their good life and orderlie conversacon maie wynn and incite the natives of country to the knowledge and obedience of the onlie true God and Saviour of mankind, and the Christian faythe, which, in our real intencon and the adventurers free profession, is the principale ende of this plantacon." [7] Efforts began at once for this " principale ende," but only very meagre results were reported for some years. The fact is, those of the colonists, in Plymouth or the other New England colonies, who took their missionary responsibility

---

[7] Quoted in Barnes, L. C., *Two Thousand Years of Missions Before Carey*, 397.

seriously were all too few; hence the small results. There were outstanding exceptions. Roger Williams must be named first, for he was " the first man who gave so much attention to the conversion of the native heathen that he can be called a missionary to them." [8] Before his removal to Providence he began work among the Indians, living among them and learning their language. After his settlement in Providence he spent much time visiting them and preaching the Gospel to them, continuing in this activity for forty years, and interesting himself both in their general welfare and in their spiritual improvement.

A better known name in Indian missions is that of John Eliot. Eliot's work was not more extensive than that of Williams but more constructive. After working among the Indians around Roxbury, where he had a pastorate, he gave himself to the Indian work exclusively, winning many to the Christian life, organizing Christian villages, training Indian Christian workers, and translating the Bible into their tongue. He prepared an Indian Grammar and an Indian Primer, and during his four decades of missionary work gathered a Christian community of more than a thousand.

Following John Eliot came the Mayhews on Martha's Vineyard Island, beginning in 1646 and continuing through five generations for one hundred and sixty years. Hundreds of Indians were converted and many churches were organized, with Indian pastors in charge.

We can find sufficient explanation of the missionary interest among the New England colonists in their genuine and deep-rooted religious life, coupled with the pressing in of the mission field upon them on all sides. They had come to America primarily to satisfy their religious needs. Their religious life was vital and genuine and was the most outstanding thing in their experience and community relation-

---

[8] *Ibid.*, 400.

ship. It was natural that they should in some degree seek to share their religious life with the people whom they found around them. And the fact that the Indians were close at hand and always to be seen would tend to press home upon their consciences more or less continually the need of the heathen people for the Christianity which they themselves enjoyed. But they had only a beginning of missionary interest. They did not go far afield. It was a very local work and very limited. It did not reach far in their own land,[9] and there is no suggestion of extending the endeavour to the less fortunate in other lands. There was the germ of the missionary idea, but it had yet a long development before it would come to full growth.

Occasional voices were raised in Europe in behalf of missions. There were some among the Dutch. In the earliest Reformation days Erasmus had called vigorously for missionary activity, but it was only an incidental call, with no campaign for its general acceptance, and no genuine evangelical basis for it. The Dutch East India Company, founded in 1602, was given missionary responsibilities in its charter. It promptly began to send out preacher-missionaries, whose duties included care of the Dutch colonists and evangelization of the native people. It established at Leyden a Seminarium Indicum for the training of these preacher-missionaries. Preaching in the native languages, translation of the Scriptures, and education of native leaders went along vigorously at first, but soon degenerated into the most shameful superficiality, people being baptized by the hundreds at so much a head. The difficulty was the lack of a genuine evangelical basis; the company, since it was the government, was assumed to be responsible for the religious life of its subjects. The Dutch churches in the homeland made no

---

[9] Of course frontier missions to white settlers were a much later development.

effort of themselves to carry on missions. Heurnius, Dankaerts and others heard the missionary call within themselves and gave voice to it in publications which they issued; but these met no response from Christians generally. Both Heurnius and Dankaerts proved the reality of their missionary spirit by becoming missionaries themselves, yet even this did not stir the Church. The great theologian and jurist Hugo Grotius published a treatise *On the Truth of the Christian Religion* to help the colonial missionary work, and it was perhaps under his influence that seven young men, jurists like himself, decided to undertake missionary service, three actually going to the field, but establishing no permanent missions.

In England, also, the missionary spirit was stirring the minds and hearts of individuals. Cromwell had a great scheme for dividing up the world into four great mission provinces, the work to be under the direction of a state-appointed central council. Alleine, whose *Alarm to the Unconverted* used to be so well known; Oxenbridge, who sent forth a *Proposition of Propagation of the Gospel by Christian Colonies in the Continent of Guyana;* Prideaux, the Dean of Norwich, who appealed to the Archbishop of Canterbury in behalf of the heathen in the English colonies, and George Fox, the founder of the English Friends, were individuals who raised their voices in behalf of missions to the non-Christian world. The Corporation for the Propagation of the Gospel in New England (1649), which helped Eliot, and the Society for the Promotion of Christian Knowledge (1698), which later rendered large service to the Danish mission in India, were permanent results of the growing missionary interest in this century.

In Germany, Bibliander the Semitist had in the sixteenth century been stirred by his studies to a realization of the need of the Mohammedans and the heathen; and in the closing years of the seventeenth century Leibnitz, influenced by the missions of the Jesuits in China, published their letters with an introduction by himself. But Bibliander had no followers, and Leibnitz thought of missions simply as a phase of Western culture.

These were some of the individual voices and efforts. Some heard clearly the missionary call for themselves, and others saw something of its meaning for Christians generally. But the old notion that the care for the religious needs of the people was the responsibility of the government was still persisting, and the Church had not yet seen that missions are an essential element in Christianity and the inherent duty of all Christians.

The first to state the missionary idea adequately and clearly was Adrian Saravia, a Dutch Reformed pastor, who spent the last quarter of a century of his life in England. From the latter country he published, in 1590, a treatise on the different orders of the ministry, which contained a chapter on missions. This was brought in to show that bishops were needed in order to plant new churches, but it led him to go deeply into the question of the authority and duty of missions. The heading of the chapter is " The command to preach the Gospel to all nations binds the Church, since the apostles have been taken up into heaven; for this, apostolic power is needed." As Saravia's treatise laid the basis for the later full expression of the missionary idea, his argument is of interest. The command to preach the Gospel to all nations, he pointed out, was not given solely to the Church of the apostolic days, but holds for every century until the end of the world. This is clear for several reasons: (1) Because with the command is given the promise, " Lo, I am with you alway, even unto the end of the world," and as the promise is for all of Christ's followers the command applies to all of them likewise. (2) Because the apostles chose and appointed

associates and successors in their missionary work, showing
that they recognized that it was only the initiation of the
work that the Lord had committed to them—it was to be
continued by others. (3) Because quite evidently the work
was much larger than the apostles could accomplish, few as
they were and brief as were their lives. (4) Because the
continuance of missionary work through the centuries since
the time of the apostles proves that the spreading of the
Gospel has actually been going on constantly among new
peoples. So that it is the duty of the Church to be still
obedient to the Great Commission and to give the Gospel to
the nations to whom it has not yet come. Power for the
accomplishment of the work has been provided, and the
Church, by virtue of the authority committed to it through
Peter, must set men apart for this task. I have already
noted the position that Beza took in replying to Saravia, as
well as Gerhard's remarkable arguments along the same line.
Their reasoning prevailed for the time being, but Saravia had
set forth the true position clearly and unequivocally.

Yet he had not gotten down to the real foundation of missions. And he was content to let the matter stand with this
one pronouncement. Three-quarters of a century were to
pass before a definite campaign for the organization of a
mission to the non-Christian world was to be undertaken.

It will be noted that Saravia, as well as all others who up
to this time had discussed the question, either favourably or
unfavourably, rested their arguments almost exclusively upon
their interpretation of the Great Commission. These verses
seemed to be everything that was to be considered in the
matter, and the sole question was whether or not they taught
that the Church had still the missionary duty. Large
numbers of present-day Christians who believe in missions
doubtless likewise rest the argument entirely upon their interpretation of these words. But the missionary idea has a

deeper basis than that, and it remained for Justinian von Weltz, an Austrian baron, to set the missionary task upon a broader and truer foundation. He, to be sure, like Saravia, gave attention to the Great Commission, but his chief arguments for missions were (1) God's desire to bring all men to the knowledge of the truth, (2) the example of those who through all the centuries since apostolic days have been missionaries among non-Christian peoples, (3) the prayers in the Lutheran liturgy that God would lead the erring to the knowledge of the truth and would enlarge His kingdom, which necessarily requires the sending out of missionaries if these prayers are to be more than simply words, (4) the example of Roman Catholics with their Congregation for the Propagation of the Faith. Here we have, not an argument from the Great Commission, but a recognition of the essential nature of the Gospel itself, God's good news that He wishes to save all men and has provided for their salvation in Christ; if we accept that and pray for the coming of His kingdom among all men we cannot avoid the responsibility of sending out messengers with the good news everywhere. That is basic. Von Weltz caught the idea that missions are inherent in the very nature of the Gospel, and that the missionary duty is not fundamentally dependent upon specific words of Jesus. Others had argued from the Great Commission: he went straight to the heart of the Gospel. And though in combating opponents he weakened his position somewhat by engaging in argument on the same old question whether the Commission was for all Christians or for the apostles only, the missionary idea had come to its own, and was now based, as it must always be based, on the character and message of the Gospel itself. It is significant that he was equally interested in both the deepening of Christian experience and the missionary expression of that experience. The relation between the two was vital.

Von Weltz sent out a preliminary publication, calling for a missionary society, then followed this with three treatises setting forth his ideas and outlining a plan for the organization of the society which should carry out his missionary ideas. There were no immediate results. The superintendent of Ratisbon warned against the proposed society with the prayer, " Preserve us from it, dear Lord God," and the ministers to whom it was presented simply laid it on the table. But Warneck sees the possibility that Spener, the father of Pietism, who came to the front about this time, may have been influenced in his missionary ideas by von Weltz.[10] And certainly the latter's conception of the missionary idea was henceforth a permanent possession of Protestantism. Von Weltz believed in what he preached, for he devoted most of his property to the furthering of his plans, and then himself enlisted in missionary service, going to Guiana and there shortly giving up his life in the work.

III

There is a straight line from von Weltz to Spener and Francke and the Danish-Halle mission of the Pietists, and through them to the Moravians and Wesley and Carey.[11] Pietism was the first broad movement in Protestantism in furtherance of the missionary idea. It was not primarily a missionary movement, but its essential characteristics led naturally into the acceptance of the missionary idea and the missionary responsibility. It was a reaction from the deadness and formalism into which Protestantism had fallen by the end of the seventeenth century, as a result of its doctrinal and polemic emphasis. As opposed to this, Pietism laid stress upon a living Christian experience and a practical expression of Christianity. It was narrow as to culture and

---

[10] *Outline of History of Protestant Missions*, 39.
[11] Schlunk, *Die Weltmission des Christentums*, 82.

theological views and ecclesiastical arrangements, but its emphasis on a genuine experience and on the translation of that experience into practice led it into the broadest application of Christianity, so that it included the whole world in its thought and its service. Add to this its Protestant inheritance, especially through Saravia and von Weltz, and we can see how it came to express the missionary idea in organized missions.

The Pietists themselves did not organize a mission. It was the Danish king, Frederick IV., who originated the plan, influenced no doubt by the still prevailing idea of the responsibility of a ruler for the religious nurture of his subjects—in this case the heathen in the Danish colonies. He called for missionaries through his court preacher, but the latter could not find any candidates in Denmark, so he turned to the Pietist leaders in Germany, with whom he had previously been associated. The result was that Ziegenbalg and Plütschau, two Pietist theological students, were appointed and the mission in Tranquebar, in southeast India, was begun. We cannot here trace the history of that mission. The significant point is that not only was the mission begun by Pietist missionaries but that all the missionaries for many years were German Pietists, appointed by Francke, who conducted the correspondence and issued the reports. " In Copenhagen the head, in Halle the heart," says Schlunk.[12] " Pietism united itself with missions, and this union alone enabled missions to live." [13] And this because the Pietists grasped the missionary idea.

Spener had seen the significance of personal Christian experience as involving missionary outreach, and had early said that " the obligation rests on the whole Church to have care as to how the Gospel shall be preached in the whole world,

[12] *Die Weltmission des Christentums,* 110.
[13] Warneck, *op. cit.,* 52.

and to this end no diligence, labour or cost be spared in such work on behalf of the poor heathen and unbelievers." [14] Francke, before the beginning of the Tranquebar mission, had proposed a Universal Seminary (1701), and the next year had founded his Oriental College. Through his schools and orphanage and the theological department of the University of Halle he sent out a great company of missionaries. How Pietism influenced the Moravians we shall see. And indeed its influence continued down into the nineteenth century in the founding of the early German missionary societies, the Rhenish, the Basel and the North German. It is evident that Pietism was missionary at its core; and that was because it interpreted vital religious experience as involving the most thoroughgoing and the widest possible practical expression. It was thus based upon personal experimental knowledge, and belonged to Christians, not to governments. Pietism ended the notion of missions as an affair of the government, and definitely grounded the missionary idea in Christianity itself and placed the missionary obligation upon Christians as such. Thus the idea developed in Pietism in two respects: it was carried back to personal religious experience, and the necessity of organization for its active expression was recognized.

But the idea was still incomplete. The Moravians added to its meaning. These humble folk were in the true Protestant succession, being followers of Huss and having been refined through persecution to a pure and vital evangelical faith. They were " men hard as steel, with iron will, ready to devote everything to winning one soul to the Saviour." [15] A little group of the remnant found their way to the estate of Count Zinzendorf in Saxony, and there consolidated their church and developed their missionary ideas and enterprise.

---

[14] *Ibid.*, 39.   [15] Schlunk, *op. cit.*, 111.

Their spirit was that expressed by Zinzendorf in his well-known words, " I have but one passion, and that is He, only He."

The Moravians were missionary before they came to Herrnhut—Bishop Comenius, as far back as 1644 or 1645, had mentioned missions with other essentials of a living Church—but their organized missionary activity came through their association with Zinzendorf. And he was indebted to Pietism for his missionary spirit. As a boy he had spent some years in Francke's home and institution, where he had heard missionary discussions and had met missionaries like Ziegenbalg and others. His grandmother, who cared for his early home training, was acquainted with Spener, who was a frequent visitor at her house. His missionary zeal developed as he grew up, and his wife stimulated his missionary purpose. And when he met at Copenhagen a West Indian Negro and two men from Labrador and heard from them of the need of their fellow-countrymen for the Gospel he was ready to lead the Moravian Christians in their missionary adventure. Pietism had given to him his deep religious experience and his missionary vision; the Moravians had a like evangelical background and missionary spirit. The result was the beginning of the unrivalled Moravian missionary enterprise.

The unique contribution of the Moravians to the development of the missionary idea was their recognition of missions as the responsibility of the Church as such. The Pietists were not *the* Church nor *a* church. Their congregations were *ecclesiolae in ecclesia*, little churches within the Church; the organized Church absolutely rejected their teachings, missions and all. But the Moravian churches accepted the missionary idea in Christianity in the most thoroughgoing way. They saw that it belonged not only to individual Christians but to the whole Church as an organization. To become a member of the Church was quite as likely to mean service in the West Indies or Labrador or Africa as in Herrnhut. The result was the missionary stream that poured forth so widely —twenty-eight fields were entered in twenty-eight years, and still others later. Out of the conception of the missionary responsibility involved in church membership grew the large use of laymen; missions were not to be a matter of an order in the Church, but something belonging to all. These missionaries were not well trained educationally, and their work consequently was often lacking in the greatest effectiveness, but they held tenaciously to that which was fundamental to their missionary endeavour, genuine Christian experience; and candidates for baptism were carefully trained and thoroughly tested. For the Moravians, vital Christianity quite naturally eventuated in missions, and quite as naturally the missionary undertaking was an affair of the whole Church.

IV

The spiritual successors of the Pietists and the Moravians were the Methodists and other evangelicals of England. It was through contact with Moravians that John Wesley gained the religious experience that fired him with his evangelistic zeal. The evangelical movement that began with Luther reached its climax in the Wesley Revival. Like Pietism and the Moravian movement, it emphasized as the central thing personal, conscious fellowship with God, a real religious experience. This was its message. Rationalism had made religion a dead thing, a matter of form and ceremony. A London advocate reported that he was unable to discover whether a preacher to whom he listened was a disciple of Confucius, of Mohammed, or of Christ. But there was no mistaking the message of the Wesley movement. And its influence went far beyond the Methodist societies which Wesley formed, into all the free churches, and into the established Church as well. So that as a result of the movement there was throughout England, and especially in the towns and villages, a throng of Christians with a surging religious life that sought for expression, and a rapidly growing group of churches in which this was the message and the life, Baptist and Independent and Established as well as Methodist.

The Wesley movement found expression in evangelism. Evangelism and missions are of course essentially the same, and the evangelism of the English evangelicals was largely home missions, reaching neglected groups with the Gospel. But of missions in the larger sense there was nothing in an organized way until Carey came. John Wesley had the missionary spirit and vision: " The world is my parish," he said, thus proving that he was in the real apostolic succession of missionary leaders like von Weltz and Francke and Zinzendorf. Whitefield, too, was stirred by missionary zeal, and urged the observing of special hours of prayer " for the outpouring of the divine Spirit upon all Christians, and over the whole inhabited earth." But there was no effort to organize a missionary enterprise or to send out missionaries abroad. Philip Doddridge among the Congregationalists tried to form a missionary society and to awaken his fellow-Christians to definite work for the people of non-Christian lands, but met no response. Baptists in 1784 sent out a call for a concert of prayer, but did nothing further. Methodists made no effort to build upon the foundation they had laid and to start a foreign mission. Thomas Coke, in 1786, began a mission to the Negroes of the West Indies, which, followed by his efforts elsewhere, finally (1813) stirred the Church at home to organized work. But his was purely an individual enterprise. The churches awakened by the evangelical movement had not grasped the missionary idea. In this the English evangelicals fell short of the Pietist and Moravian movements.

What, then, was the contribution of the evangelical movement in England to the development of the missionary idea?
Directly it contributed nothing. But indirectly it made the
largest possible contribution. It vitalized all those factors
which were to issue in the broad missionary programme of
Carey, such as exploration, trade, humanitarianism and
learning, giving them a purpose that turned them to use in
the making of modern missions. It laid a missionary basis
of fervid religious experience in groups of Christians in
many communions throughout England. It provided the
leadership for the later missionary movement, in Carey
and others. It is impossible to overestimate the importance
of the Wesley evangelical revival in preparing the way for
the great missionary undertaking that followed and in
making it possible. But it can scarcely be said that the
eighteenth century evangelical movement in itself added
anything to the developing missionary idea. The larger
development was to come in Carey, the product of the
evangelical revival.

V

And so we come to William Carey, rightly called the
founder of the modern missionary movement. He was by no
means the first missionary of modern times, nor was his society the first organized missionary effort. What, then, is his
significance? First, the society which he organized was the
first distinctively foreign mission organization. The Wesley-
ans, as I have said, had had missionaries, but their work had
been simply personal efforts; the Moravians had carried on
their mission as a Church; the Indian missions in the English
colonies in America had been really home missions; and the
Society for the Propagation of the Gospel, while founded
with a foreign mission aim, had actually up to this time been
a colonial society, limited to work in the Western Continent.

Carey's society united a *group* of Christians and churches, it was an *organized* effort, it had a distinctively *foreign* mission aim, and it led immediately to *other* similar societies with similar organization and aim. Secondly, Carey's mission was the beginning of permanent work in a large field. The Moravians had small fields, lacking in far-reaching significance; the Danish-Halle mission was limited to a small territory, represented Francke and the Halle group rather than the Danish churches, and was not permanent in any extended way. Carey's mission had the broadest possible aim and outreach and was permanent both in itself and in other missions that followed. Thirdly, in Carey's work are defined the leading principles of modern missions, such as native leadership, a strong centre with outstations, interdenominational fellowship, social ministry, wide circulation of the Scriptures, the fundamental place of evangelism. This was of immense significance. Fourthly, the greatness of Carey himself, as a man and as a leader, makes him of historic importance. Richter rightly recognizes this when, in his *History of Missions in India*, he heads the section dealing with this period " The Age of William Carey." His perseverance and patience, his poise and humility, his tact and irenic spirit, his love and Christian devotion, his broad scholarship and his statesmanlike grasp of the missionary problem, all mark him as a figure far outstanding above all who had preceded him, with none greater among those who have followed.[16]

Not to underestimate the unique personal factor, Carey was largely the product of historical forces that found their culmination in him. I have dealt with these in their general

---

[16] " There has perhaps been no missionary equal to him in India. There have been very few who have not been inspired by his example." Arthur Mayhew, *Christianity and the Government of India*, 113.

relations elsewhere.[17] We are here concerned with their contribution to the development of the missionary idea of Carey.
In this development we can trace four factors that were influential. One was the voyages of Captain James Cook, the
account of whose explorations, particularly in the South Pacific, were eagerly devoured by Carey. They gave him a
broad knowledge of the world, and an intimate acquaintance
with the people of neglected lands. Out of his reading came
his handmade leather globe and the map that hung on the
wall of his cobbler's shop. But the significance to him of
these peoples made known by Cook and others was expressed
in the exclamation that is said to have burst from him frequently when with his globe he was teaching geography—
" They are all heathen! They are all heathen! " This
attitude was the result of other factors, among which must
be mentioned the Bible study in which he was constantly engaged. He knew his Bible well, and saw the significance of
those passages that brought out the missionary purpose of
God and the missionary duty of His people. His famous
*Inquiry into the Obligation of Christians to Use Means for
the Conversion of the Heathen* begins with a section setting
forth the teaching of the Bible on the subject, and their application to the world situation. His epoch-making sermon
on the text Isaiah 54:2, 3 was simply the culmination of his
studies that carried him into the Old Testament as well as
into the New. His knowledge of the South Seas people and
his interest in them became focussed on their spiritual desti-
tution through his reading of the Scriptures, and the recognition of their need included a recognition of a like need
elsewhere. Of course we go back of his Bible study to the
Wesley Revival for a third factor in his missionary development. This was really primary, for it was in Hackleton
Meeting, one of the humble products of the Wesley move-

---

[17] Chapter 5.

ment, that he was converted to Christ, and gained that spiritual purpose that gave him his missionary interest. And it was also out of the evangelical movement that his dominating evangelistic purpose came. Finally, as a fourth factor we may group the sermons and missionary appeals that culminated in his own response, Andrew Fuller's sermon on " The Gospel Worthy of All Acceptation," and the Scottish call to prayer, taken up by Jonathan Edwards in America and finally sent out in England by Carey's own Northampton Baptist Association.

From these factors, and from the larger world movements that came to focus in him, we can understand the elements in his missionary idea. It is clear that Carey understood missions to be the duty of all Christians. We see that in his repeated appeals to his fellow-ministers and to the churches. It stands out in his thoroughgoing treatment of the question in the *Inquiry*. It comes to a head in his offering of himself for the work, though he could not have thought of himself—and did not—as having apostolic qualifications. But as he saw his own missionary duty it was clear, for it belonged to all Christians. He saw, too, however, that all Christians did not recognize and accept the task, and hence there was included in his idea the voluntary nature of the service. The Church might be a missionary organization, as in the case of the little Herrnhut church of the Moravians, but where churches and Christians differed in their attitude toward the question, as in England, a society apart from the Church, or rather within the Church, was necessary, in which membership should be voluntary. And no one could be compelled to undertake missionary service: here, again, it was a voluntary matter. But if missions called for a voluntary service, that was not to leave God out of account. In his missionary idea God was central. If he recognized the aid of discovery and government and transportation and learning, it was evident to him that these were means that God had used and was using, to open the way for His people to accomplish the great task committed to them of making Him known to all peoples.

The *content* of his missionary idea was large and all-inclusive. Evangelism was fundamental and central. This stands out in his appeals for the organization of the enterprise. It was constantly emphasized in his letters. The first article of the Serampore Covenant was " To set an infinite value on men's souls." Evangelism was his constant practice, even when he was teaching and translating in Fort William College. His missionary idea included also making the Bible known universally. Hence his feverish endeavour to provide translations in all the languages of southern Asia. Next to the spoken message was his emphasis on the message of the Word itself. Then with this came his inclusion of education in the missionary idea. Through this means he would provide native evangelists trained to interpret the Scriptures and to lead the growing Church, men who would be broad in their knowledge and faithful in their search for truth, while they laid chief stress upon mastering the Bible. His breadth of interest brought social ministry into his missionary idea also, and led to his activity in ridding India of age-long evils like the drowning of children in the Ganges, suttee, and slavery. Finally, his clear grasp of the missionary idea brought into that idea a wide interdenominational fellowship in missionary service. He was a Baptist, but he saw that the pioneer work that constitutes Christian missions makes possible and imperative the co-operation of all who hold to the central things of Christ and His Gospel. " Every public institution aiming at India's betterment," he said, " ought to be constructed on so broad a basis as to invite the aid of all denominations."

Carey, then, greatly enriched the content of the missionary

idea; he made basic the evangelistic purpose in missions; he built his missionary organization upon the principle of voluntary enlistment; he placed the responsibility for carrying the Gospel to all the world upon all Christians; and he based his missionary idea, like von Weltz and the Pietists, on the whole purpose of God as revealed in Scripture and on the experience of God that we have in Christ. Such was Carey's missionary idea.

VI

The missionary idea did not end its development with Carey; it is still growing. So to complete our study we must look at the idea as we see it today.

Its content, immensely broadened by Carey, has become still richer. The wall of separation between home and foreign missions has to a considerable extent been removed and our missionary idea includes both as essential parts of the one idea and purpose. Government, business, travel, and other occupations are seen to have the most intimate relation to the missionary enterprise, and we are beginning, rather vaguely, to include in our missionary idea their Christianization. We recognize phases of truth in the non-Christian religions, and we are seeking to adjust our attitude to them in such a way as will bring into our missionary idea a close relation of Christianity to these non-Christian faiths. Thus far our grasp of this relation is not clear, and the result among some students of missions has been vagary of thought that tends to cut the nerve of missions.

The missionary idea has still only a limited acceptance. Efforts for the widening of its acceptance have become immensely greater in number, in variety, in studied planning, and those who are acquainted with the missionary task are probably much better informed than were their fathers, while probably the number well informed is greater than ever before. But the proportion of members of Christian churches who accept the missionary idea for themselves is still exceedingly small; only a minority have it as a dominating purpose in their lives. Those who accept the missionary idea recognize it as of universal application in the Christian Church, but the idea has yet to be grasped by the great majority. And this applies not only to the Church at home but in large measure to the Church on the mission field. One of the great problems facing Christian leaders in mission lands, and one that is far from being widely seen and appreciated, is to instill into the minds and hearts of the Christians the missionary idea in its fulness. Many churches among the nationals are evangelistic, but relatively few are missionary.

What still prevents the full acceptance of the missionary idea? Many things could be named; we have hardly space to do more than list them. First can be mentioned nationalism, an exaggerated patriotism and egoistic self-complacency that makes much of the importance of one's own country and nation and has little thought for the value of others. Closely related is race antagonism, found widely among those who are otherwise Christian, and raising a barrier between individuals and groups and races that effectually prevents missionary interest or a fundamental friendliness. A third obstacle is secularism, influential not only outside the Church but in it, making us blind to the spiritual needs of the world in our emphasis upon human life and activity apart from God. Astonishingly common in this apparently well-informed age is a narrow mental outlook, which is a fourth difficulty in the acceptance of the missionary idea. Newspapers with a lack of due proportion in importance of emphasis govern the mental attitude of the great majority, and relatively few read books that challenge thought and widen outlook. Churches could hardly render a larger service in the formation of the missionary attitude than to widen the mental—

and at the same time the spiritual—outlook of their members. The final obstacle, and the fundamental one, is the dull spiritual experience widely prevalent. The only source of missionary interest, as I have frequently pointed out in tracing the development of the missionary idea, is a genuine religious experience in fellowship with God. Only in this can the missionary idea find root. Where it is lacking, and to the extent to which it is lacking, the missionary duty will not be accepted. Fundamentally, the way to the full acceptance of the missionary idea is along the line of its development in the thought of von Weltz and his successors, the deepening of the religious consciousness and experience. That which is central in Protestantism, the personal fellowship with God in Christ, is what must be stressed most of all. It is this idea, central to Protestantism and central to the Gospel, which will yet bring the whole Church to accept the missionary idea.

V

THE SOURCES OF MODERN MISSIONS

EVENTS do not happen. This is as true in history as in chemistry or physics. Back of all the great episodes and facts in the history of the world's life there were movements and events out of which they inevitably grew. History is a chain of cause and effect. The relation of this to missionary history was discussed in the first chapter. Missionary movements have always been the result of causes which, in part at least, we can trace. To discover and explain these causes and their resulting effects is the work of the historian. The causes as well as the effects are important for any one who is to understand the history of the missionary enterprise, or the meaning of the great epochs in that history. We are now living in one of those epochs, one which began with William Carey. It is easy to think of him as simply a man who in the providence of God was raised up to lead in the inauguration of the modern missionary movement. We are not by any means to leave out God—all history is of His making. But Carey and his movement were the result of factors and forces which God used. Carey was the culmination of definite movements in that great period which began with the Protestant Reformation. We may think of him as standing at the focus of certain forces, the meeting-place of many streams. What some of these streams were we can clearly see.

I

One of the streams of influence was exploration. The

story of exploration is a fascinating one, full of bold adventure, heroic effort, persistent faith, thrilling events, not to overlook the cruelty and selfish ambitions of many of the adventurers. The Portuguese were the leaders, under Prince Henry the Navigator and his successors. Seeking for a new route to the rich lands of the East they pushed steadily down the west coast of Africa, until in 1497 Diaz reached the Cape of Good Hope, and ten years later Vasco da Gama sailed around the tip of the continent and on to India. Other voyagers travelled down the east coast of Africa. In 1500 Cabral, sailing westward, reached Brazil. Still other explorers followed in da Gama's track and raised the Portuguese flag in Ceylon. Others pushed still farther east, and finally reached the Spice Islands. By 1511 Portugal had spread far across the world.

Spain was not much behind its neighbour Portugal. Columbus reached San Salvador in 1492 and the American continent in 1498. Balboa crossed the Isthmus of Panama in 1513 and looked out upon the Pacific Ocean. In 1519 Magellan started on his world-encircling voyage, and though he himself lost his life in the Philippines, one of his lieutenants, del Cano, completed the circumnavigation of the globe. Cabrillo reached the California coast in 1542. And many other Spanish discoverers sought and found new lands in East and West, or like Cortes and Pizarro extended Spanish dominion in the lands made known by others.

Next came the French. The Pope had divided the new world between Spain and Portugal, but neither France nor Holland, nor indeed England, cared for that decision. France sent Verrazano to the North American shores in 1524, and ten years later Jacques Cartier explored the St. Lawrence River. The French were not particularly active in original discovery, but they followed others in valuable explorations, as when Champlain journeyed up the St. Lawrence Valley, and LaSalle and Marquette opened the vast Mississippi Valley to the world.

The Dutch tried to find a northeast passage along the roof of the continent north of Europe, though without success. But around the turn of the sixteenth century they had a notable succession of explorers in the Pacific, within half a century taking most of Portugal's possessions from her, and adding discoveries along the coasts of Australia, New Zealand and other shores. A notable name in American exploration was Henry Hudson, an Englishman in the employ of the Dutch, who placed on the map the bay and river that bear his name.

Last came the English, with Cabot making his noteworthy discovery of the North American coast in 1497. Other familiar names are Frobisher and Gilbert, and the best known of all, Francis Drake. The latter's freebooting expedition down the South American coast and around Cape Horn made the world acquainted with the western shores of America and enriched the coffers of Elizabeth.

By 1700 almost all the world's coastline was known. And already exploring had led to colonizing. Settlements were made by Portugal in India, Africa and Brazil; by Spain in South and Central America and the Philippines; by France in Canada and India; by the Dutch in New Netherlands, Guiana, South Africa, the East Indies and Ceylon; by the Danes in the West Indies and India; by the English in North America, the West Indies and India. Some of the colonists went out just for adventure, to see the world, to enjoy the novelty of a new kind of life, and perhaps to have some exciting experiences. Some went because they were down and out, or were politically ostracized, or were criminals exiled by the government. Others sought for gold, or trade, or wealth in some other form. Still others went as representatives of their rulers, to enlarge the national territory and expand the national life. And finally, there were those who were adventurers for religious freedom or who crossed the seas to win the newly-found peoples to the Christian faith.

In general there was little religious or missionary interest in the colonies. The settlers in New England were mostly an exception—though as a matter of fact not all of them by any means were really Christian, or eager for the spread of the Gospel. There were some other exceptions, like the Friends, and later the Moravians, in the middle colonies, who had strong religious life and engaged in missions to the Indians. And in French Canada the Jesuits, with monks and nuns of other orders, impressed religion upon the daily life of the people in the settlements, and gained a fairly strong popular support for their missionary undertakings. Spain, on the other hand, never established colonies in the real sense, and the Spanish settlements, full of adventurers and gold-seekers, were not encouraging centres for the heroic efforts of the early Roman Catholic missionaries. In India and the East the great trading companies ruled, and none of them was genuinely favourable to missions, being afraid that religion and business would not mix—at least not to the advantage of business. The colonists were almost all connected with the work of the company, English or French or Danish or Dutch, and had little religion of their own and none to spare for the natives. There were noble exceptions among the colonists, and there is a brief missionary story to the credit of the Dutch East India Company, with a meagre one in the history of the British Company; but by and large the new settlements were not centres of religious life nor very favourable bases for missions.

Nevertheless the explorers and the colonists blazed a trail for the missionaries. Exploration was of high importance as a factor in the making of modern missions. To begin with, the explorers opened new lands for Christian enterprise, and made known new peoples for Christianization. They told strange tales of the customs and religious life of the natives, and stirred the interest of some at home. Some of the rulers recognized their responsibility to these new heathen subjects of theirs, and the missionary orders of the Roman Church promptly took up the work of making the new-found peoples Christian. The story of the great orders is a story of fascinating heroism and devotion, though of mistaken method and ideals. But the significant thing is that it was the explorers who stirred the friars and the Jesuits to the carrying on of missionary endeavour. Exploration became a fruitful source of Roman Catholic missionary effort. The Protestants were slow to respond to the opportunity which the colonies offered, but gradually opened their eyes to the vision that the new world spread before them, and at last answered the challenge as the Roman missionaries had begun to do earlier. The notable fact is that but for the explorers there would have been no missionaries, for there would have been no mission lands or peoples of whom they would have known. The missionary enterprise owes this great debt to the adventurers and explorers.

Another significant result of the exploring movement was that it opened new routes of travel. That was, of course, particularly true as respects the Far East. Before the fifteenth century trade was carried over the long highways that stretched across Asia. Those who travelled used these land routes. But they were very difficult—there were no roads such as we know, or even such as the Romans had built across Europe—and they were dangerous. Moreover, after the Crusades they were in the hands of the Moslems, and it was almost impossible for others to travel them, or indeed even to reach them from Europe. But the discovery of a sea route to the East revolutionized travel to that part of the world. The way of the sea might be a dangerous one, but it was as safe as the way of the land, and it was surer, for it was not controlled by the Moslems, but was open to all. Africa, too, was made accessible by the new explorations. Hitherto the mighty Sahara had shut off travellers completely from the continent to the south. The voyages of Diaz and da Gama and others showed a way to reach the wonderful lands along the coast. So, too, towards the golden West. With the establishment of the colonies well-known routes were opened across the Atlantic, and those who would could travel over them. Peoples who had been known very vaguely, or were quite unknown, could now be reached. And what is true of the sea is true of the new trails opened through the new continents. Pizarro laid highways for the Dominicans and the Jesuits. Champlain and LaSalle prepared the way for the missionaries to the Indians. In later decades the Protestant missionaries began to use the newly-opened routes. A most notable illustration of the service that exploration has rendered to Christian missions was given in more modern times by Livingstone, whose travels spread wide open the heart of the Dark Continent to the heralds of the Gospel. But his is only one name in the list. It was a great and unexpected service that was rendered to missions when the explorers and the colonizers opened the new thoroughfares of travel across the world.

The discovery of new lands and peoples also broadened the outlook of the Christians at home. Not that a great many of them thought in terms of the new Christian opportunity—it took a long time for the Church, especially the Protestant Church, to be awakened to that vision—but they began to live in a larger world, and that was the most valuable sort of a preparation for missionary interest. The trouble still with too many Christians is that they live in too small a world. It would be a great stimulus to every Christian to have a map of the world hung before him on the walls of his home or his church, so that he could be constantly reminded of the great world in which he lives. It was bound to widen the interest of the members of the churches at home to be hearing tales of the life beyond the sea, and to have some of their friends or perhaps their own family go out to live in the new colonies. Sooner or later, here and there, Christian people would be led to think of their Christian responsibility for those new colonies and for the heathen people there. When that feeling should become widespread, and should grip the heart of some leader, like Francke or Zinzendorf or Carey, then the Protestant missionary enterprise would be born. But the preparation was necessary, and the gradual widening of the horizon of the world in which Christians lived was one of the factors in that preparation.

Even more significant in the relation between exploration and missions was the fact that the story of those who were adventuring for gold and trade stimulated actual Christian adventure. Not only was there a vision of a larger world, but many had a vision of a larger duty. Where the explorers went, there the missionaries would go. Wherever new lands were opened, the bold friars or the equally brave Jesuits sought a place of service. So we have the stirring tales of the Jesuit missionaries in Paraguay and Canada and Goa, of the Augustinians and others in the Philippines, of the Franciscans in California; and in the Protestant story the thrilling adventures of the humble Moravians, the stirring story of John Williams in the South Seas, and the feverish response of the Church Missionary Society to the appeal of Stanley for missionaries to Uganda, as well as the eager enlistment of Christian forces for Japan as soon as that land was opened to foreigners. The missionary enterprise is indebted to the adventurers through many centuries for the inspiration for its task.

Still another point of significance for the development of the missionary movement is found in the fact that the colonies became bases for the evangelization of the native peoples. The settled centres to which the missionaries went were of immense help to them—and this in spite of exceptions like the Danish colony at Tranquebar, whose governor hindered Ziegenbalg and Plütschau in every possible way, and the attitude of local officials of the British East India Company in Calcutta and elsewhere. It was natural that the missionaries should go to the colonies. There they would find an orderly government, protection would be furnished if needed, supplies could be secured for their work, the people spoke their tongue or one that they could understand. It was to the colonies that the vessels sailed that were to carry them to their work, and in the colonies they might perhaps secure the help of co-workers. The story of missions is very intimately connected with the story of colonization. Father Fleche in Champlain's settlement in Nova Scotia, Francis Xavier at the Portuguese colony of Goa in western India, George Schmidt in Dutch South Africa, the Danish mission sent at the instance of King Frederick IV. to Tranquebar, the chaplains that accompanied Cromwell's expedition that made Jamaica a British colony, the choice of India as the field for Carey's epoch-making missionary beginnings—these are illustrations from the story of the missionary pioneers. Almost invariably they made a colony their base, and from that as a centre worked far out into the interior. From these many points of view the work of exploration was one of the fundamental factors in the making of the modern missionary enterprise.

II

Trade was another such factor. The chief aim of the explorers was to establish routes of trade. There were some, as we have seen, who went for treasure, and some who went just for the thrill of going, but the great commanding purpose of the princes and kings and queens who paid the expenses of the exploring expeditions was to open a way to the East and thus secure a share in its rich trade; or to find a route to the West and establish a monopoly of the trade in the new world. It was this that led Prince Henry the Navigator to send his ships down the African coast, it was this that stirred the imagination of Columbus and drew him forth on his great adventure, it was this that brought Champlain to Canada and Hudson to New Netherlands, and carried Magellan and del Cano on their world-encircling voyage across the Atlantic and the Pacific from Spain around to Spain again. As a result of the voyages and discoveries a new world of commercial possibilities was opened to the peoples of Europe, and they were not slow to take advantage of it. Trade grew rapidly. New foods appeared. New articles of apparel were to be had. New wants were developed. And commerce spread from Europe to the ends of the earth. The growth of trade during the sixteenth century was so great that it has been spoken of as " the commercial revolution." [1]

Out of this great trading movement grew the famous trading companies, of which " The Governor and Company of Merchants of London Trading into the East Indies," in other words the British East India Company, is the best known though by no means the only one. These chartered companies were established by almost every European country. There was one or more for nearly every section

---

[1] Hayes, *Political and Social History of Modern Europe.*

of the new lands east and west. Besides the British East India Company, the French, the Dutch, the Danish and others had companies with a monopoly of trading privileges in the East. And there was the Company of New France, the Dutch West India Company, the London and Plymouth Companies, and others. Their aim, the aim of them all, was trade, business, profits. What Warneck, with but little exaggeration, says of the British East India Company could largely be said of all: " It sought gain, always gain; every idea higher than a money standard was alien to it." [2] With their business privileges they combined rights of government, and though the parliaments and courts at home held a veto power and not infrequently gave their commands in unmistakable language, the companies were practically supreme. Their attitude toward missionary effort, therefore, was most important and influential. And it will be readily understood that with so strong an emphasis on profits as Warneck's quotation suggests, there was not likely to be much interest in missions. The British East India Company was not unwilling that its chaplains should do a limited amount of missionary work, provided it could keep it well in hand, that is, hold it subordinate to its aims for money-making. But to a general missionary enterprise, uncontrolled by them, the British Company, as all the companies with scarcely an exception, were vigorously, often violently, opposed. [3] The experience of Judson and his companions in being expelled from India by the government is illustrative of the attitude of that company and of most of the others. Where there was not open opposition there was indifference, as in the case of the Dutch East India Company, which, like the British Company indeed, had in its charter a provision

---

[2] *Outline of a History of Protestant Missions*, 78.
[3] Mayhew, Arthur, *Christianity and the Government of India*, Pt. I.

for carrying on missionary work, and which began faith-
fully, soon to lose interest in the enterprise, however, and
to do nothing of a genuine character in missionary effort.
Indeed, the giving up of its Seminarium Indicum because
the graduates gave too much attention to the evangelization
of the natives is an indication and illustration of the fundamentally unfavourable attitude of the Dutch and other
trading companies toward missions. But, as we shall see,
these great trading organizations nevertheless became important factors in the development of the modern missionary
enterprise.

It was natural that the companies should develop the
keenest rivalry. They wanted a monopoly of trade in the
countries where they had established colonies, but several
occupied the same territory or were close neighbours. They
had powers of government, they maintained military forces,
and it was easy to come into collision with each other.
Conflicts between the company armies drew the home governments into conflict. Sometimes the rulers in Europe
themselves began the strife. Sooner or later all the countries having trading companies engaged in war with one
or another of their rivals; but the outstanding struggle for
supremacy was that in which France and England engaged.
It was a long contest, culminating in the middle of the
eighteenth century with the victory of the English in Canada
and India. This victory of England was not only important
in its economic and political results: it was most significant
for missions. The substitution of a Protestant for a Roman
Catholic power laid the foundation in Canada for the strong
base of missionary expansion which Canada has since become. In India it brought Protestants in increasing numbers into the country as rulers and potential friends of
missions and as missionaries themselves. Moreover, the
British people at home, who were Protestants, became inter-

ested in India as their own territory, and the Christians among them could not but recognize, ultimately, the responsibility which the possession of this great missionary territory placed upon them. And not least in importance was the fact that when they finally did turn their hand to missions there was a great field available for them to which they were most intimately related. What is said as to the importance to Protestant missions of the supremacy of Protestant England in India applies likewise to the supremacy of Protestant Holland in the East Indies. Had Portugal or Spain retained the control the missionary history of those islands would have been vastly different. The opposite situation in South America, with the resulting religious history, is significant in this connection.

The culminating feature of the trade movement in these centuries—the sixteenth, seventeenth and eighteenth—was the Industrial Revolution in England. Apart from economic and social factors the causes were the inventions which made possible improved and increased product in manufacturing, such as the power loom, the spinning mule and jenny, and the cotton gin, and the successful application of steam to manufacturing and transportation. The result was an immense increase in manufacturing and the changing of England from an agricultural to a manufacturing country. Busy factory villages sprang up, towns came into prominence, and some of the towns rapidly developed into cities. A middle class of manufacturers and business men appeared, who became promoters of culture and learning. Canals and roads brought the people together, and the rapid increase of manufactured goods and the need for increased raw product resulted in great expansion of shipping.

The whole trade movement, and especially the Industrial Revolution, formed one of the most significant factors in the development of the missionary enterprise. First of all, like exploration, it provided an acquaintance with non-Christian peoples. The many new articles of food from the new lands, the things to wear that were brought from over the sea, these and other things brought it about that the large number of folk who were in one way or another connected with manu-facturing and trading had their thought turned constantly to the lands from which the raw products came or to which the finished articles went. The whole trading movement tended to expand the mental outlook of the people and to broaden their knowledge and interest. And not the least element in this expansion of outlook was the personal knowl-edge gained by many who were sailors or traders and who made the voyage to the new lands themselves. Foreign trade made America and the Indians, India and the Hindus, household words in England.

A middle class, as we have seen, grew out of the develop-ment of the commercial and trading movement. The impor-tance of this to missions is not hard to see. The middle class, made up principally of the manufacturers and commer-cial men and their families, became the group that supported and promoted missionary work. This is the class on which the enterprise largely rests now, and it rested on it then. And the manufacturing villages and small towns were the centres where missionary interest was to be found. It was among the factory population of the midland counties that the organizers and supporters of the first societies lived. Witness Carey and Fuller and their associates. When the leaders of the Baptist Society went up to London to enlist the co-operation of the Baptists of the metropolis they met a cold reception; the movement arose in the villages and towns, the manufacturing centres, the home of the new mid-dle class. Here was the stronghold of the evangelical move-ment, here were the aggressive commercial men, and here the effort to Christianize the new-found peoples took root.

Moreover, as I have pointed out, culture and learning were promoted by the commercial men. They established libraries and institutes, such as the Leicester Institute from which Carey gained so much, and thus broadened the knowledge and widened the outlook of large numbers of people. Thus they helped to lay the foundation of interest on which the missionary enterprise was built.

The new acquaintance with the non-Christian people in India and elsewhere, gained through trade, and the response of the commercial men and traders to the challenge of the new opportunity, tended to arouse in church members a sense of their own Christian responsibility for those people. The moral response answered to the commercial response. Not that there was an immediate uprising of the churches comparable to the commercial revolution—that, of course, was not at all the case—but the influence was at work, and after a while it was to issue, with other influences, in definite effort for those who were thus brought to their attention through trade.

An outstanding result of the development of trading colonies, the organization of the companies, and the growth of foreign trade was the providing of ample means of transportation and communication. The trade routes meant regular lines of travel. The companies had to have plenty of ships, and these were available to a greater or less extent for missionary travel and the shipping of missionary supplies. To be sure, the opposition of the British Company to missionary effort prevented Carey from sailing on one of their ships, and made it necessary for Morrison to go to China by way of America, but even so they did go finally in trading ships, Carey in a ship of the Danish Company and Morrison in an American trading vessel. So also in the case of the Danish missionaries to Tranquebar and the Dutch missionaries to the East Indies; they were able to make use of the facilities for travel provided by the companies of their own lands. Others for the most part travelled the same way, Roman Catholic missionaries to Canada, Moravians to the West Indies. War vessels were sometimes used, but of course there were no passenger liners; trade furnished the facilities for travel and shipping and mails. It is difficult to over-emphasize the importance of this factor. One can sense something of the service provided by the companies to the missionaries by trying to imagine what the situation would have been had there been no such facilities. It is hard to see how missionaries could have reached their fields; at least they would have had very long delays, even longer than what they did sometimes experience. Transportation and communication were provided for missions by the growth of trade. And the Industrial Revolution, immensely stimulating trade abroad, added proportionately to the shipping and other facilities that were made available.

III

A third source of the modern missionary movement is to be found in learning and the spread of knowledge. The seventeenth and eighteenth centuries set before us a galaxy of great lights in the firmament of learning. Newton and Huygens in physics, Boyle and Lavoisier and Rumford in chemistry, Newton, Galileo, Kepler, Laplace and Herschel in astronomy, these are only leading names in a long list. Knowledge which in the Middle Ages had been limited by its strictly moral emphasis, and which in the Renaissance had been enriched by the treasures of the ancients, now was set free entirely to seek truth wherever it could be found. The theory of education was broadened. Bacon brought out the inductive method in England and Comenius developed it on the Continent. And the natural result of this free search for truth was the development of popular education. Schools grew in number and were made available not only for those of high social station but those of low degree as well. In the manufacturing villages as well as in the cities schools were established. And other educational agencies were added; newspapers began to be issued in England about the beginning of the eighteenth century and rapidly grew in number and circulation; libraries were opened and institutes and forums were founded. The result of all this was a wide spread of learning, and the development of a spirit of open-mindedness toward new ideas, both of which played their part in preparing the way for the missionary undertaking.

The modern educational movement, so briefly sketched, had great significance for missions. In the first place, there was the broader knowledge of the world which came to the common people, and to the people in general. This was not mere hearsay or rumour or common talk. It appeared in books of geography and history and travel, in reports and published letters, in the wealth of information and new ideas that schools and libraries and institutes and newspapers brought to the minds of the people. Carey's leather globe, from which he taught his pupils about the people of distant continents and far-away islands of the southern seas, is an excellent illustration of the way in which this popular knowledge was broadened. Of course, without knowledge there could be no interest, but with the wider and more intensified knowledge that came to the people of England there was laid a broad foundation for the appeal which was to come to them to send the evangel to other peoples. Especially did the broader and more hospitable attitude of mind which the newer learning fostered become a factor in opening the minds of the people to such bold new plans and projects as the missionary undertaking.

A second result of modern learning that was favourable to missions was the development of educated leaders among

Christians. It is significant that practically every great movement for advance in the world's history has been led by one who had thorough education. Especially can that be said of the advancing history of Christianity. Paul, Columbanus, Luther, Loyola, Wesley, Carey, Judson—these are illustrations. So far as modern Protestant missions are concerned this was particularly significant, as that movement grew up largely among the humbler folk, who in an earlier generation would have produced no educated men. They would have been led by those without education, and the movement would have lacked wise organization and development. But the wide spread of learning provided the new movement with trained leadership, and thus made a contribution to it in a field of the greatest importance.

A third element of significance in the relation of learning to the modern missionary enterprise is to be found in the fact that the universities became centres of missionary effort. Not to mention Paris, whence came the Society of Jesus, one thinks of Halle, the home of Pietism and the centre of the Danish-Halle mission, as well as the source of missionary influence among the Moravians through Zinzendorf; Oxford, where the Wesleys and Whitefield studied and formed their " Holy Club," the precursor of the Wesley Revival out of which came the missionary societies of Carey and his followers; Williams College, where Rice and Mills and their companions held their Haystack Prayer Meeting and formed the society of The Brethren for the promotion of a missionary undertaking, a purpose which became a reality in the American Board of Commissioners for Foreign Missions and the Baptist Triennial Convention. In France and Germany and England and America learning thus made a contribution of the utmost significance—how great it was appears as we consider the part that the universities and colleges have played in the missionary enterprise since those days, as suggested by such names as Duff, the Universities Mission in Africa, and the Student Volunteer Movement for Foreign Missions. In these and other ways learning proved a most important source for modern missions.

IV

There were other streams of influence that contributed to the making of the missionary enterprise of modern days. One might mention nationalism, closely connected with exploration and colonization, yet a distinct factor. And humanitarianism, arising in France with no Christian interest whatsoever, but spreading to England and arousing the Christians of that land to their responsibility for giving the best they had for the enrichment of the life of others. But we must content ourselves here with one other factor, the most important of all, evangelicalism.

When we turn back to the beginnings of evangelical faith in the Reformation we are struck with the almost entire absence of the missionary idea. This I discussed in detail in the previous chapter. The significant thing, as I pointed out, is not the lack of missionary effort but the lack of missionary interest: it was not in the thought of the Reformation leaders and there was no expression of regret that opportunity or resources did not make a Protestant missionary enterprise possible. But as we saw, in the evangelical life and message of Protestantism there was the basis, the germ, from which missions would develop in time.

If there was no missionary interest in the sixteenth century there was little to be looked for in the seventeenth. This was a century of formalism in religion. The warm evangelical life of the earlier days had cooled and a religious life succeeded it that had no vitality and spiritual experience and hence no outreach of missionary thought or effort. But towards the end of the century a reaction followed in the direction of vital religion. Pietism arose, emphasizing real experience on the one hand and a practical expression of that experience on the other. Thus the Pietists had the necessary spiritual basis for missionary effort and a definitely practical attitude which gave them an interest in such an undertaking. Out of Pietism grew the Danish-Halle mission in India, and through Francke its missionary interest reached Zinzendorf and the Moravians. In the Moravian Church we have another high point in the development of the evangelical factor, contributing to missions its principle of the identity of church membership and missionary duty and the example of high consecration to actual missionary work on the part of its members. To this must also be added its influence upon Wesley and hence upon Carey and his associates.

The Wesley Revival was the culminating phase of the evangelical movement which we are tracing. In the England of the eighteenth century religious life was again at a low ebb. The court was notoriously corrupt; society was honeycombed with immorality; thought was largely dominated by French atheism or by deism; the Church's religious life was stagnant and utterly lacking in vital religious experience. As William Jay said, " The establishment was asleep in the dark and the dissenters were asleep in the light." Against the background of such conditions the Wesleys and Whitefield preached their Gospel of personal salvation and real Christian experience. The results are well known. A moral and religious transformation spread through England, evangelical churches sprang up everywhere among the middle class, the free churches were revived, and an evangelical group arose within the established Church. The influence reached America and even the Continent. And the leaders, like John Wesley, had an active missionary interest, growing out of their emphasis upon vital religion. The movement was essentially missionary.

We do not need to trace the history of the evangelical movement in greater detail, for it is generally familiar. Moreover, the previous chapter, on " The Development of the Missionary Idea in Protestantism," largely supplements what is said here. Among all the factors that made for the development of the modern Protestant missionary enterprise evangelical religion is to be considered supreme. Viewing the whole movement from Luther to Wesley, we can see, first of all, how it vitalized all the other factors. Humanly speaking, apart from exploration, trade, nationalism, humanitarianism, learning and the rest, there would have been no Protestant missions. But with them all there would have been none except for the evangelical movement. It gave life and Christian influence to all the others and made them *actual* missionary factors instead of merely *potential* factors. More definitely, evangelicalism furnished the germ for a sure missionary development. Even though the Reformation leaders did not sense the missionary implications of the Protestant faith, that faith had within it what was bound to express itself ultimately in the widest missionary outreach. The real religious life which it emphasized, in distinction from any imagined salvation by sacerdotal magic, was certain to lead those who had this experience to share it as widely as possible; and with its Gospel of ecclesiastical freedom it was sure sooner or later to break forth in such broad missionary effort as was seen in the Pietist movement, the Moravian Church, the Wesley Revival and the Missionary Society of William Carey.

Again, the evangelical movement provided actual examples of missionary endeavour, which would tend to encourage further and larger effort. There were individual missions on the part of some who caught the missionary significance of the evangelical faith, like Peter Heiling in Abyssinia, von Weltz in Guiana, and workers among the Indians in America

such as Eliot, Brainerd and the Mayhews. There were societies that had an early part in American missions, the New
England Company and the Society for the Promotion of
Christian Knowledge. There was the organized mission of
the Danish government and the Halle Pietists in Tranquebar, and the gathering stream of Moravian missionaries with
such names as Zinzendorf, Nitzschmann and Dober, and
David Zeisberger. And there was the British Society for the
Propagation of the Gospel in Foreign Parts, practically a
colonial society but with a basically missionary aim. It
would not be probable that these would be unknown to
evangelical leaders, or that they would be without influence
on their attitude and outlook. To be sure, the influence was
long in gathering force, and other influences were needed,
but nothing is more powerful than example. Doubtless von
Weltz's personal enlistment in the missionary undertaking
was quite as influential as his treatises, and the sight of a
little church like that of the Moravians at Herrnhut giving
itself with such unanimity of devotion to the missionary
cause must have aroused evangelicals elsewhere to inquire
as to their own responsibility for that cause. We know how
John Wesley was affected by his contact with the Moravians; it may well be that the missionary impulse that we
have said was a characteristic of the Wesley Revival was the
result, largely, of that contact and influence. Without doubt
the examples of missionary enlistment given by evangelical
leaders and groups strongly reinforced the idea that the
evangelical faith was essentially missionary and developed
the germ of missionary growth which was within it.

Finally, the evangelical movement laid the basis for the
organization of modern Protestant missions in the evangelical churches which resulted from it in England. It was
from these churches among the non-conformists or in the
Church of England that the leaders of the missionary move-

ment came. Carey and Fuller were pastors of such churches among the Baptists and organized the Baptist Missionary Society; Philip Doddridge, as pastor in Northampton, gave the initial impulse that later resulted in the London Missionary Society; the Church Missionary Society represented the evangelical group in the Church of England: and the early missionary societies in America and Germany were founded by those who were stirred by the same movement of revival. The evangelical stream did not spend itself in the awakening of individuals; but through individuals it resulted in the founding of churches with the missionary spirit, the reviving of denominations and the awakening of their missionary responsibility, and at last the organizing of churches and individuals into the missionary enterprise for which so long a preparation had been making.

Here are the streams out of which came the modern missionary movement, the highways that led to Kettering and Carey. Those who travelled along the highways—the explorers, the traders, the scientists, the humanitarian leaders, the evangelicals of the early days—could not see whither they led. We from our mountain peak can look back across the world of history and see that at the end of the highways stood Carey. He was the heir of all the contributions of those who had come along the thoroughfares of the past. It is easy, looking at Carey, to see in concrete ways how those influences which we have been tracing built themselves into the making of Carey himself and of the enterprise in whose initiation he was the chief figure.

The explorers had made India known, and that became his mission field. The trade movement had built the manufacturing villages where he lived and preached and where the churches were to which he appealed in behalf of his missionary undertaking, it was trade that had made India a great colony and had brought it under the British flag, it was in a trading ship of the Danish East India Company that he sailed to India. Learning made its contribution to him through Wesley and others, and notably in the Leicester Institute where he read and studied and conversed with more learned men. Finally, evangelical religion contributed to the making of Carey in his conversion in Hackleton Meeting and in the training which came to him at Moulton and at Leicester. It was an evangelical group of churches and leaders to whom he turned in his missionary plans. His was an evangelical message, and beyond all his work as translator and teacher and reformer and scientist must be remembered his passionate and ceaseless evangelism, that gripped him so powerfully that his biographer could say of him that "when he had no conversions he was like a woman craving a child but knowing no motherhood." [4] The evangelical movement had implanted in him the deep religious life which gathered together all the other contributions of the centuries and turned them into one supreme effort to win men everywhere to Christ and to make life everywhere Christian.

[4] Carey, S. P., *William Carey*, 180.

VI

THE AUTHORITY FOR CHRISTIAN MISSIONS

TWELVE hundred years ago! It was the heyday of Christianity in Asia. Christian bishops in all the large cities throughout the continent. Christians among the Turks, the Afghans, the Tibetans. Christian churches in China and Burma and Siam. Christian hymns in Mongolian and a dozen other Asiatic tongues. Through ten centuries of evangelism Christianity was carried across Asia by the Nestorian Church, heretics in relation to Rome, splendidly orthodox in relation to the Great Commission, " the most missionary Church the world has ever seen." [1] It stirs one's imagination to read the story. How tragic that persecution and compromise should later wipe out the Christian faith from practically the whole of the great continent, leaving hardly more than inscriptions and traditions to tell us of those wonderful early centuries. But through the years other streams of missionary effort have poured across the world. And now again in Asia, and indeed in almost every land in every continent, the Christian Church has its missionaries, telling to those of other faiths the story of the Saviour born in Bethlehem, crucified on Calvary, risen as a living hope—the Saviour and the hope of all the world.

It is a marvellous story, this story of Christian missions. Nothing in all history equals it—a story of adventure and

---

[1] A. Mingana, John Rylands Library, Manchester, quoted by Stewart, *Nestorian Missionary Enterprise*, 88.

faith and abounding love—the story of the greatest and most successful work of the Christian Church.

I

There is plenty of thrilling interest in the story, and lessons without number for us and for our twentieth century Christian enterprise. But the question has to be asked, What authority, after all, has Christianity for its missionary undertaking? It is a question that cannot be avoided. For the right of Christians to disturb those who already have a religious faith is being challenged by many thinking people. Some who raise the question are inside the Church; not all are outside. Many Christians question the propriety of our going to others with a Christianity that we have so imperfectly realized ourselves. And there are not a few who doubt whether our Christian faith ever will or ever can dominate the world.

Consider the present situation. Money is lacking for missionary work. To be sure, more is being given than formerly, but in view of the increased cost of missions—as of everything else—there is scarcely more money available than before the World War. Indeed, in many churches in recent years the most strenuous—sometimes almost frantic—efforts have been necessary just to keep the standard up to the previous year, to say nothing of advance. This is a situation all too familiar.

Consider the lack of prayer for missions, in church and home. The missionary movement was born in prayer. The apostles looked to the prayer life of the Church for stimulus and power. The prayer lists in the Fraternity Books of the eighth century monasteries were used constantly by Boniface in Germany and by others in England in their evangelizing of the people. It was through the concert of prayer that the churches of Britain were prepared for William

Carey's challenge and the resulting missionary enterprise. The prayer-meeting under the haystack at Williams College started the American churches on their world adventure. And there are multitudes still who support the missionary work of the Church by their prayer. Except for their prayer missions would die. Yet it cannot be said that the Church is enthusiastic about missionary prayer. You can go for weeks to many a church and seldom hear a prayer for missionaries, for the Christians of mission lands, or for the awakening of the Church at home to missionary earnestness.

Moreover, there is a lack of conviction as to the ultimate success of Christianity in its missionary endeavour. We read of the " mistakes " of missionaries in the past, of the " failure " of missions in China or India or elsewhere. We are asked, " Have not missionaries done more harm than good? " The present success of missions is doubted, and the future success as well. Even certain of the preliminary studies for the Jerusalem Conference seemed to accept this attitude, appearing to favour a co-operative search for God —Christians with Hindus or Buddhists—as though Christianity were not to be expected to supplant other faiths.

So far as territorial advance is concerned, missions are largely marking time. There has hardly been any forward movement into new areas in a generation. The thorough-going survey of unoccupied fields prepared as a preliminary study for the Jerusalem Conference apparently received no consideration by the Conference and does not appear in the published Report. The emphasis has almost wholly changed from geographical expansion to intensive Christianization. The latter is important, beyond question, but meanwhile millions of men and women are untouched by Christian influence and have no knowledge of a Saviour. The challenging watchword of the Student Volunteer Movement, " The Evangelization of the World in This

Generation," no longer stirs with its urgent appeal either youth or adults.

All of this situation—our poverty in money, in prayer, in faith, in adventure—means that there is lacking an intense conviction of the need of the world for the Christian Gospel, as a necessary, exclusive, supreme way of salvation and of life; in other words, a weakness in the sense of authority for Christian missions.

Four reasons suggest themselves for this lack of conviction, this doubt as to the right and duty of Christians to propagate their faith. One reason is the new attitude toward the peoples of the East. We have come to a new appreciation of their culture, their great literature, their historic civilizations, and their wonderful achievements in our own time. As between the Orientals who are here among us and the bulk of their Occidental associates, we see no difference morally. So our conception of their spiritual need, all too commonly based on the externals of life, loses its intensity and its urge. We have accepted the notion that the religion of non-Christian peoples is of the same high character as the culture that we admire, and we do not sense its woeful lack of moral ideal and of saving spiritual power.

Indeed, our whole attitude toward those of other religious faiths has radically changed. Our fathers believed that those who died without having heard of Christ were eternally lost. One remembers an address in which the speaker emphasized the great multitudes who because they had never been told of Christ were passing out of this life into eternal separation from God. Holding his watch in his hand, the speaker counted off the seconds—" one, two, three, four, five, six "—and one could almost see these lost souls as one by one they passed out into the dark forever. It was a tremendously gripping appeal. We do not hear appeals like that today. Not many now believe that those who through no fault of their own have lacked the opportunity of knowing Christ are thus condemned from the presence of God. It is more commonly held that God in His infinite love takes account of the differing circumstances of life, and accepts those who are obedient to the law written in their hearts, and to that imperfect revelation of God which they have. This belief has tremendously affected our sense of the urgency and authority of our message. The tragedy of a soul separated from God in eternity is gone; the equal tragedy of a soul separated from God in this present life does not grip us. So the authoritative command to go and preach the Gospel to all peoples loses its urgency and imperative.

A second reason for the present situation is the secular interpretation of life, due in part to the scientific dominance of life and thought. Unconsciously this has affected the attitude of Christians. Science certainly does dominate our life. The auto, the airplane, the printing-press, the movie, the discoveries of medicine, the almost human machinery in our factories, the ever increasing inventions and manufactures that flood our stores and crowd our homes—these testify to the place that science has in our everyday life. We have accepted the evolutionary interpretation of life, and in spite of theistic affirmations by many outstanding scientists we have largely left God out of the process. I repeat these words, for they explain our situation and our attitude—*we have left God out of the process*. That is to say, we have in great measure adopted a non-religious interpretation of life, and do not feel deeply either our own need for God or the need of people elsewhere for Him. *Material things* dominate us, rather than *spiritual ideals*. Science is a method of thought; we are trying to make it an ideal for life. Civilization, culture, trade, education—these we gladly carry or send to the peoples of the whole world; but God, Christ, salvation from sin, do not stir us to a like missionary service and sacrifice.

A third reason for our lack of belief in the authority of the Christian message is our doubt as to what the Christian message really is. There is strong contention and vehement debate regarding the essentials of the Christian Gospel. There are parties in our denominations and opposing groups within our churches. Periodicals carry frequent articles on the Christian message, with confusingly different interpretations. Moreover, in many of the sermons to which Christians listen there is lacking a positive message; the dogmatism of the past is happily gone, but the strong conviction whose place nothing can take is not always in evidence. So the positive assurance of the message of Scripture as God's message, of the Christian Gospel of salvation as the *only* Gospel and the *only* salvation, does not grip the hearts and lives of Christians as they need to be gripped, to make them feel the need of all men for that Gospel and that message. Thus lack of conviction as to the message weakens the sense of the supreme authority of our message.

The three reasons that have been given for the weakened conviction as to the authoritativeness of Christian missions apply more or less to the churches of both the West and the East. But so far as Western Christianity is concerned a fourth reason must be added. I refer to the luxury that characterizes our personal and social life. Luxuries have become needs, extravagances have become necessities. This has centred our thought upon ourselves, and has turned our attention away from others. After caring for our own wants we have not money left to provide a doubtfully needed service to people twelve thousand miles away. *Our* needs appear so great that we do not sense the needs of others in a compelling way. Hence the weakness of the missionary appeal.

II

What is the aim of Christian missions? This is a root question when we inquire into the authority for the missionary enterprise. Authority for what? What are we trying to do?

The history of the missionary expansion of Christianity presents a changing expression of the missionary aim. The aim of Paul and his missionary successors was almost wholly evangelistic—the winning of individual disciples and the organizing of these into churches. Some bit of social work in the apostles' day is suggested by the directions given for the care of widows, the advice as to the healing of the sick, and the warnings against the dangers and injustices of wealth. But evangelism was the chief thought, both in apostolic times and in the days immediately succeeding. A beginning was made a little later in organized theological education, as in the important school of Pantænus at Alexandria, but of other forms of education we hear little or nothing. Provision was widely made for education in the countries adjacent to the Mediterranean, and the social needs and opportunities in these lands had not yet pressed themselves upon the attention of the Church. Moreover, what we know of missionary efforts in Britain, Abyssinia, Persia and India during these early centuries supports the view that in this period of missions evangelism was practically the exclusive aim and method.

The next great period, from the fifth to the twelfth centuries, was devoted to the Christianizing of Asia and Europe. The destruction of the widespread Christianity in Asia has left us but a meagre knowledge of the missionary methods employed. Evangelism was most prominent, but education had a recognized place, translation and other literary work received emphasis, and some attention was given to the building of a Christian society. Of the methods and aims of the missionaries in Europe we know much more. The characteristic missionary instrument of both Romans and Celts was the monastery. Recall what has been said in previous chapters as to the monasteries and their significance. In that period, it will be remembered, the monastery was not a place of retreat from the world, but a training-school for missionaries and evangelists, and a centre for religious culture, evangelism, education and industry. Missionaries who went out from one of these monastic training-schools founded other similar institutions, from which the evangel was carried into all the country near and far. Within the monastery the monks gave themselves to Bible copying and translating and other literary activities. All around there grew up a Christian community, with industries of various kinds fostered by skilled leaders from the monastery. Evangelism and Christian teaching were central, but literary, educational and social work held an important place. In the midst of the culture of the Mediterranean lands there was no insistent demand for Christian civilizing efforts; but the ruder life of northern France and central Germany presented vividly the need for a broad Christian service, and the methods and the aim were correspondingly more comprehensive.

In the next period, that of the early Protestant missions before Carey, evangelism was again the dominant, almost sole method. Justinian von Weltz, the seventeenth century Austrian baron who was the first Protestant to call the Church insistently to missionary effort, set forth in his treatises the duty simply of preaching the Gospel among the heathen. The Pietist movement of the seventeenth and eighteenth centuries was distinguished, as we have seen, by its emphasis upon the inner religious experience, and the Danish-Halle mission, manned by men of the Pietist school, while broadening the aim a little, in general hewed close to the line of evangelism. So, too, the Moravians, who united two lines of evangelical influence, the Unitas Fratrum of Bohemia and the Pietism of Germany, in missions that have had uniformly almost an exclusively evangelistic aim.

The modern missionary movement began with the broadest possible expression of missionary interest in Carey, who added to his unbounded zeal in evangelism his never-equalled series of Bible translations, his scholarly educational work, his social reforms, his translations of Indian classics, and his scientific researches. Yet in this varied ministry Carey was first of all an evangelist. " To set an infinite value upon men's souls " we have quoted from the covenant of the Serampore trio. Through his busiest days he spent his Sundays and three days a week in outdoor evangelistic work. " I hear you speaking of Dr. Carey, Dr. Carey," said he to Duff on the last visit of the younger man to the great pioneer; " when I am gone, say nothing about Dr. Carey, speak about Dr. Carey's Saviour." Thus is expressed the central and fundamental aim in Carey's missionary plans.

Professor Richter, of Berlin, names the first two periods of modern missions in India " The Age of William Carey " and " The Age of Alexander Duff." [2] Carey, translator, educator, social reformer, scientist, was as we have just seen first of all an evangelist. Duff, scholar and teacher, had likewise pre-eminently an evangelistic aim. To use his own words, he wanted " to prepare a mine which should one day explode beneath the very citadel of Hinduism itself." Following Duff came a host of others, with widely differing methods. Judson in Burma was an evangelist and a translator of the Scriptures, Martin in China was a teacher, Ashmore was an evangelist; Verbeck in Japan was educator,

[2] *A History of Missions in India*, 128, 173.

statesman, translator; Mackay of Uganda was engineer and
evangelist, Chalmers of New Guinea was an explorer and a
preacher. And so the story goes, a many-sided activity,
hardly two missionaries doing exactly similar work. What
impresses us most in the historical expression of the missionary aim, as we note it in the methods employed, is its variety, depending on differing conditions and differing needs, in
the changing life of many centuries and many lands.

But we have now come into new times. In the missionary
world we are face to face with new conditions. There is a
new social interest. Peoples that were long content with
things as they were are now examining their customs, relationships, social structure, frankly facing the moral questions involved, and seeking ways of improvement. There is
a *new intellectual enthusiasm*. Schools are crowded and
overcrowded. Adult education is an organized movement.
The spirit of studious criticism is widespread. The best in
knowledge and thought is sought from all the world. There
is a *new breadth of religious appreciation*. In the old religious communities reformed groups have appeared. New
religious movements have sprung up. Among many earnest
souls there is even a deep interest in Christ and in His teachings. There is a *new spirit of secularism*. The value and
validity of religion in any form is denied by many. With
not a few leaders, Christian and non-Christian, the contest
has shifted from Christianity vs. Hinduism, or Christianity
vs. Buddhism, to religion vs. secularism, faith vs. agnosti-
cism, and there has been a drawing together of Christian
leaders and leaders of other faiths in what has seemed to
some of them a common problem and challenge.

Out of these new conditions have arisen new methods of
Christian work. New emphases have appeared. And the
question presents itself anew, What is really the aim of
Christian missions? Is it to reform and ennoble and purify

social relations and ideals—to instil into these the spirit of
equality, of service, of freedom, of love? Is the aim the
enriching of men's minds—stirring up the thought-life of
young men and women and helping to develop and train
leaders equipped with mental power, moral earnestness and
breadth of view? Are we, in other words, to try to persuade
followers of other religious faiths to interpret their religion
in terms of Christ's ethical teaching? Or, on the other hand,
are we to insist that salvation of heart and life, and spiritual fellowship with God, are possible only to one who
accepts and follows Christ, to the exclusion of all other
religious loyalties? Or shall we hold to a middle ground,
and believing that " he that feareth God and worketh right-
eousness is acceptable to him " (Acts 10:35), whatever the
name by which men call Him—Allah, Vishnu, Jehovah,
Father—join with seekers after Him in every faith in the
development of personal religious experience and in a common search for God?

An increasing number of critics of the older attitude put
the question bluntly, " Shall we Christianize or proesly-
tize? " One writer entitles his article, " Converts or Co-
operation," [3] and says, " The issue comes to the fore whether
the missionary can continue to be a missionary in the accepted sense of the word, namely, a proselytizer, endeavour-
ing to persuade men of other religious faiths to enter into
the fellowship of his own. For some, the orthodox position
is becoming increasingly difficult. . . . The missionary issue
has shifted from converts to co-operation." This expresses
an attitude that not a few are holding.

In the midst of this new situation, and of this confusion
of voices, can we discover a true and abiding aim in Christian missions? I am sure that we can. In all the varying

---

[3] *The Journal of Religion,* April, 1928.

expression of the missionary aim through nearly nineteen centuries, the one great outstanding purpose has been to offer to others, whatever their religion or religious attitude, the *Christian* Gospel, the unique message of *Christianity*. That aim still remains the aim of the Christian missionary. By whatever methods or in whatever forms we may express it, the essential aim is to give the *distinctive Christian message* to all people. Christianity has enriched our lives and the lives of all peoples who have accepted it. That enrichment we must make the possession of still others. If there are followers of other faiths who are searching for God, we shall sympathize with them and encourage them, but we shall not join in their search, for in all humility yet in all confidence we know that we have found God in Christ. If there are some good things in other religions—as of course there are—we shall not be blind to them, but shall gladly recognize that God has been seeking other human hearts in other lands as He has sought our hearts; yet we shall not depreciate our own experience of God as we have found Him in Christ—we shall boldly try to bring others, whatever their present faith, to the knowledge of God that we have, and to the more complete life in Him toward which we strive. The aim of the early missionaries still remains ours. As Christians, we have a unique message to give to the world.

III

What is our message? What are the unique elements in Christianity? What have we to give to others that they do not have? What can Christianity present to those who in other religious systems are earnestly seeking for God? What can we offer in the Christian Gospel which no other faith can offer—which none but Christianity has?

If we are to discover the unique message of Christianity we must compare it with the best in the messages of the other faiths. Note some of the high truths that are found in them. Islam teaches in an emphatic way the unconquerable power of God, and the supreme duty of loyalty to God's will. Hinduism keeps before us the immanent presence of God, and in its popular form offers salvation through faith. Buddhism teaches the inescapable and eternal influence of life and thought. Confucianism reminds us that we live in a world of human relationships, and summons us to a recognition of the moral duties involved in those relationships. Even animism, lowest of religions, gives constant testimony to the reality of spiritual forces and the certainty of life after death. All of these teachings, to be sure, are in Christianity, and we treasure them as part of the message of our Christian Gospel. But the important thing to note is that they are also part of the gospel of Islam, the gospel of Hinduism, the gospel of Buddhism, the gospel of Confucianism, the gospel of animism, as well as of the Gospel of Christianity.

On the other hand, there are definite fundamentals in which Christianity stands apart from all other religions. One of these unique characteristics is the quality and reach of the Christian teachings. If Islam teaches the supreme power of God, Christianity teaches that that power is united with an unconquerable love. If Hinduism teaches the immanent presence of God, Christianity shows that the immanent God is revealed in the perfection of His character in Christ. If Buddhism teaches that every act and thought has an unending influence, Christianity transforms the hopelessness of this doctrine into the bright shining of hope: to be sure, " the wages of sin is death," but Christianity adds " the free gift of God is life." If Confucianism teaches a fine code of practical ethics, Christianity shows how one can have power to transmute those ideals into life. We need not blink the fact that all the non-Christian religions have much that is noble, but we shall be blind if we do not see that Christianity goes a second mile in even the best of their teachings, and gives to them a quality and an application that is essentially unique.

But we can go farther. What gives to the Christian teaching this higher quality? There is but one answer, Christ. It is Christ Himself Who makes His teachings unique. It is Christ in Whom those teachings are unmistakably revealed in life. Christ explains the teachings of Christianity. Christ *is* the truth of Christianity. The supreme fact of Christianity is Christ. And Christ is unique. If you place by the side of Christ the founders or leaders of other religions —Mohammed, Krishna, Gautama, Confucius—great as they are they fade into the commonplace compared with His excellence. They all reveal imperfections of character. You and I know men and women who in one or another characteristic are better than they were. But Christ stands before us perfect, matchless, complete, " the crystal Christ." Said Saddhu Sundar Singh to a Hindu professor of philosophy who asked him what he had found in Christianity which he did not find in the religions of India, " I have found Jesus Christ." No other religion has a Christ.

The highest point in the revelation of Christ's character is reached at Calvary. In the Cross we see His divine self-sacrificing love in all its perfection. And here is a third element of uniqueness in Christianity's message: no other religion has a Cross. Mahayana Buddhism has the idea of self-sacrifice in the temporary renunciation of Buddhahood by the boddhisattva for the sake of helping and saving other men, but this on its moral side falls far short of the holy love of the Cross. In Krishna, Hinduism gives us the picture of a saviour who is ready to save all who yield themselves to him, but it is the holiness of Christ that gives meaning to His sacrifice of love, and holiness is not in one's vocabulary when one speaks of Krishna. Confucianism has no suggestion of a Cross of self-sacrificing, saving love, for salvation, so far as it is needed at all, is a matter of ceremony and of social ethics. As to Islam, the possibility of a Cross, in the Christian interpretation, is unthinkable, for any adequate idea of divine love for sinners is quite out of harmony with the conception of Allah. And so of other religions. Nowhere is the Cross to be found except in Christianity. It stands unique in the Christian message.

The message of Christianity, then, though in many of its teachings duplicated in one or another of the non-Christian faiths, offers at least three things which none of them gives: (1) unequalled riches of moral idealism in the teachings of Christ, (2) a revelation of the highest love and holy self-sacrifice in the Cross of Calvary, and (3) above all, Christ Himself, " unequalled by any other person who has ever lived upon earth, yet possessing the qualities of personality which all persons should possess." [4] In these three features Christianity stands apart from all other religions. None other can offer the perfect teachings of Christ. None other can present the perfect love of the Cross. None other has as its ideal the perfect personality of Christ. Here are the unique essentials of our message. To give this message to all the world has always been the aim of Christian missions. It is still their aim.

IV

We have reviewed the present missionary situation and have noted the Church's lack of missionary passion and the absence of any strong advance movement in the missionary enterprise. We have pointed out that the situation seems to be occasioned and largely caused by the new attitude toward

[4] Hume, R. E., *The World's Living Religions*, 275.

non-Christian peoples and religions, by the widespread secularism arising in a measure from the scientific dominance of life and thought, by the contention as to the real nature of the Christian message and the lack of authoritative preaching, and by the selfish luxury which seems to us a first necessity. We have inquired as to the objective of Christian missions, as shown by the methods and activities of leaders in earlier days and in the new conditions of today, and have seen that the aim has historically been to give to all peoples the distinctive Christian message. What the unique characteristics of that message are we have sought to discover by comparing briefly the message of Christianity with the messages of other faiths and have found three unique elements, the higher moral quality of its teachings, the revelation of divine holy love in the Cross, and the perfect personality of Christ. That brings us to our final question, which is the question with which we began, What is the basis of authority for the Christian missionary enterprise? What right have we Christians to carry the distinctive message of our faith to those who already have a religion of their own? The answer has been implied in our discussion of the aim and message of missions, and only a brief word is here finally needed.

It will be evident that this basis of authority does not lie in the assumed possession of a superior civilization or culture. Who is to decide what civilization or culture is superior? What is the standard by which cultures can be accurately or impartially measured? Certainly Christianity is not identical with Western civilization—factories, sewing-machines, modern farm machinery, European dress, American school curricula, democratic institutions. These may be of great value, but they are not Christianity. Paul was quite as good a Christian as though he had woven his tents on a Jacquard loom. Paul the Apostle of the Congo did not live in a modern apartment house, but in an African hut, yet he was mighty in his knowledge of Christ. The failure of the early missionaries in the South Sea Islands is a significant illustration of the true principle enunciated by Carey, " Not civilization first and then Christianity, but Christianity the royal road to a worthy civilization." Our authority does not lie in the civilization that is ours.

Nor is the possible contribution which missionaries can make to the education of the peoples to whom they go the basis of authority for their work. Education has a proper place in missionary method. History makes that clear, as we have seen. The Christianizing of the processes of thought and the motivation of knowledge by unselfish Christian purpose are necessary factors in the making of an indigenous Christianity. But the essential thing is Christianity, not knowledge; first an experience of Christ and a thoroughgoing loyalty to Him, then the application of this experience and loyalty in the realm of knowledge and thought, as in every other realm.

Not even in the power to relieve suffering or to release from poverty is to be found the essential authority for missions. From the example of Christ we have ample justification for all social service. Such service is essentially Christian. We need more of it in missions rather than less. But this is not basic. It is result, not cause; a necessary corollary to the fundamental principle.

Where, then, is the authority for the missionary enterprise? Fundamentally it rests upon the imperative demand of truth for universal proclamation. Truth requires utterance—it cannot rightly be kept hidden. Knowledge is a universal right—it belongs to all. Whoever possesses what he believes to be the truth is bound by the truth itself to make known the truth to others. It is in accordance with this principle that Professor J. F. McFadyen has emphasized the identity of the missionary idea in religion and other phases of life.[5] As he points out, the man who writes a book is a missionary in behalf of the truth he is presenting; the teacher is a missionary and has back of him the authority of the truth he claims to teach. In the same way the Christian has the authority of truth for his missionary endeavours. This is not to assume that the Christian alone has the right to carry on a mission in behalf of his religion; the Buddhist has an equal right; so has the Moslem and the Theosophist. But that which gives to any one, Christian or other, the right to give to others the message of his faith is the belief that his message is the truth. No one has a right to withhold from others what he deems to be high and valuable truth. So that if we believe that in Christianity we have truth possessed by no other religion, we have a right, and not only a right but an inescapable obligation, to make that truth known, to spread our message of truth, and to enlist all persons, all peoples, as followers of Him Who, as we believe, spoke truly when He said of Himself, " I am the Truth." The dilemma of Archbishop Whately cannot be avoided: " If my religion is false I ought to change it; if my religion is true I ought to propagate it." The demand of truth is the fundamental basis for the authority of Christian missions.

We can carry this further: the possession of anything that our experience shows is valuable gives us the right and obligation to share it with others. In this way the farmer who raises useful crops, the manufacturer who produces an article valuable to the user, the inventor and the discoverer who have found something helpful and useful, have the right to market their goods and carry them to the people of other lands. How much more have Christians the right to

---

[5] See on this part of the discussion his valuable little book, *The Missionary Idea in Life and Religion.*

make known that which has proved in their experience to have supreme value, beyond all other good, beyond things of clothing or food, beyond comfort, beyond money, worth dying for, above all other possessions worth living for—the personal religious experience found in Christ. Of course, if this experience has not proved the most valuable thing—if it takes second place, or third, or last place—it is not to be expected that its imperative will be strong. And conversely, a weak imperative, a lack of missionary constraint, a failure to feel with Paul " Woe is me if I preach not the gospel," implies an acknowledgment that Christianity, as it is known in one's own experience, is not of supreme value to oneself, not valuable enough to wish that others should have it. But if the experience of Christ is invaluable to us, and if we believe that this invaluable experience is possible in no other faith, the unselfishness that is inherent in Christianity requires us to be missionaries, and to make known to all others our own unique and infinitely valuable experience.

What we have thus presented as the basis of missionary authority, namely, the possession of what is believed to be the truth, and the experience of what is felt to be of highest value, can be summed up in one word, Christ. For us the perfect expression of truth, and the central fact of our highest experience, is Christ. For one who follows Christ, His words, His missionary command, are sufficient authority. The ultimate missionary obligation, however, does not rest— as many suppose it rests—upon detached verses of Scripture, even though these are the words of Christ, but upon Christ Himself, the incarnation of His words, His Gospel, His revelation of God. Back of His missionary command and the missionary implication of His Gospel is the imperative of His unique character and His unique personality. Here, as we have seen, is the supreme distinctive message of Chris-

tianity. Christ, Christianity's unique possession, is the final
authority for Christian missions.

The aim of Christian missions remains what it has been
through all the history of the enterprise: the presenting of
the distinctive, unequalled, message of Christianity to all
men everywhere. The uniqueness of our Christian message
consists pre-eminently in the unrivalled reach of its moral
and spiritual teaching, the revelation of holy, redemptive
love in the Cross, and the supreme and perfect character and
personality of Christ Himself. The authority for Christian
missions lies in the demand of truth for the universal proclamation of what we believe to be our unique possession in the
teachings of Christianity, in our experience of what we
count of highest value to ourselves in the Christian life, and
in our conviction that Christ is that truth and the source of
that experience. These demand our loyalty and compel us
to be missionaries. Backed by such belief and such authority we have supreme confidence in the sure and ultimate
success of the Christian mission.

INDEX

Adaptation of missionary to task, 39
Afghans, 27, 173
Africa, 19, 21, 28
Aidan, 34, 35, 61, 70, 76, 97, 107, 115
Aim, missionary, 13, 179, 183
Alleine, 132
America, 16
American Board of Commissioners for Foreign Missions, 166
Animism, 24
Annals of the Four Masters, 10
Annals of Ulster, 10
Ansgar, 32
Attractiveness of missionary, 36
Angles, 60
Ashmore, William, 181
Attitude toward non-Christian faiths, 176
Augustine, 61
Augustinians, 120, 156
Authority of Christianity, 29, 178, 188, 189

Bangor (Ireland), 62, 66, 67, 76, 78
Bangor (Wales), 57, 67
Baptist Missionary Society, 162, 169, 171
Baptists, 141
Baptist Triennial Convention, 166
Basel Society, 138
Beginnings of missions, 23
Benedictines, 77, 105
Beza, 124, 134
Bible, 55, 58, 60, 68, 76, 78, 92, 105, 108, 115, 117, 146
Bibliander, 132
Boniface, 34, 37, 41, 64, 85, 97, 98, 104, 107, 111, 113, 114, 174
Book of the Lover and the Beloved, 36
Brainerd, David, 39, 170
Brebeuf, 41
Brendan of Clonfert, 41, 57, 59, 68
Brigid, 67
Britain, 15, 57

British East India Company, 157, 158, 163
Britons, 61
Brittany, 62
Brown, Samuel R., 39
Buddhism, 16, 24, 48, 186
Burmans, 24
Burns, William C., 36

Caedmon, 73
California, 40
Call, missionary, 97
Calvin, 124, 127, 128
Carey, William, 11, 32, 34, 38, 39, 41, 45, 122, 136, 142, 143, 150, 156, 162, 165, 166, 169, 171, 175, 181, 189
Cedd, 35, 72, 73, 74, 115
Celtic monks, 10
Central Asia, 27, 28, 47, 48
Ceylon, 47
Chad, 35, 72, 73, 115
Chalmers, James, 39, 182
Character, 42
Charlemagne, 108
China, 17, 21, 24, 47
China Inland Mission, 51
Church, 30, 31, 34, 88, 108, 118, 139
Church buildings, 111
Churches, free, 83
Church home, 12, 44, 45, 95, 148
Church, Irish, 45, 48, 83, 86, 109
Church Missionary Society, 156, 171
Church, native, 12, 26
Church of the East, 45, 53
Church, Roman, 15, 37, 45, 48, 53, 64, 83, 84, 109, 110, 128
Church union, 34
Ciaran, 65, 66
Cities, 28
Clonard, 57
Clonfert, 57, 68
Clonmacnois, 57, 65
Clough, John E., 36, 37
Cochin China, 47
Coillard, François, 39
Coke, Thomas, 141

Colman, 76
Colonies, 153, 157
Colonization, 14
Columba, 32, 41, 57, 59, 61, 65, 66, 68, 96, 103, 104, 105, 110, 114
Columbanus, 37, 41, 62, 63, 64, 76, 96, 102, 105, 106, 111, 113, 114, 166
Comenius, 139
Comgall, 32, 57, 59, 66, 69, 76
Complacency, 31
Concentration, 117
Confucianism, 185, 187
Congo, 33
Co-operation, 34
Copts, 24
Corporation for the Propagation of the Gospel in New England, 132
Cosmas, 47
Cromwell, 132
Crusades, 16, 41, 154
Cujus regio ejus religio, 56, 124, 127
Cultural resources, 33

Danish East India Company, 163, 172
Danish mission, 11, 132, 136, 157, 168
Dankaerts, 132
Derry, 57
Dober, 170
Doddridge, Philip, 141, 171
Dominicans, 120, 155
Duff, Alexander, 11, 32, 34, 38, 167, 181
Durrow, 57
Dutch East India Company, 131, 153, 159
Dutch explorers, 152

Eastern Church, 16
East Indies, 161, 163
Eata, 35, 72, 115
Education, 19, 31, 33, 91, 117, 179, 189
Edwards, Jonathan, 145
Egede, Hans, 41
Eliot, John, 90, 130, 132, 170
Enda, 57, 64
England, 60
Erasmus, 131
English explorers, 152, 171
Evangelical movement, 15, 18, 167

Evangelism, 36, 48, 82, 102, 116, 141, 146, 179, 181
Expansion, 117
Exploration, 14, 150

Factors in missions, 14
Fabricius, 36
Faith, 43, 44, 89
Fernandez, 49
Fields, mission, 12, 23, 25
Finan, 76
Finnian of Clonard, 57, 63
Finnian of Moville, 57, 65
Fleche, Father, 157
Fox, George, 132
France, 21, 37, 63, 80
Franciscans, 17, 120
Francis of Assisi, 39
Francke, 136, 138, 156, 168
Fraternity Book, 106, 174
Frederick IV., 137
French explorers, 151
Friars, 40
Fullan, 81
Fursey, 59, 63, 79, 103

Gall, 63, 78, 102, 103, 111
Ganges Valley, 24, 47
Geddie, John, 35
Gerhard, 124, 134
Germanus, 55
Germany, 37, 63, 126, 132, 138
Gilmour, James, 38
Glendalough, 57
Goa, 156
Governments, 17, 21, 31, 47, 107, 126
Great Britain, 21
Greenland, 41
Guatemala, 40

Hannington, James, 40
Havana Congress, 27
Heiling, Peter, 169
Heiu, 72
Hepburn, James, 36
Herrnhut, 170
Heurnius, 132
Hilda, 72
Hinduism, 24, 186
Hübmaier, 128
Huguenots, 126
Humanitarianism, 15, 167

Ideal Christian life, 90
India, 19, 33, 153, 160, 161, 171
Indians, American, 121, 130, 153
Industrial Revolution, 161

Industry, 21, 105
Iona, 10, 59, 61, 67, 68, 85, 104
Ireland, 15, 35, 53, 56, 114
Irish missions, 33, 35, 37, 53, 61, 64, 86
Islam, 187
Italy, 64, 114

Japan, 11, 17
Jerusalem Conference, 175
Jesuits, 11, 17, 33, 37, 41, 133, 153, 154, 155, 156, 166
John Cassian, 87
John of Monte Corvino, 40
Judson, Adoniram, 34, 41, 159, 166, 181
Jutes, 60

Karens, 24, 47, 48
Kells, 34, 57
Kimura, 36

Lahus, 48
Laos, 24
Latin America, 19
Leaders, 26, 30, 33, 34, 40, 48, 56, 113, 115, 119, 165
Learning, 14, 164
Leibnitz, 133
Leicester Institute, 163, 172
Lerins, 87
Libraries, 165
Lindisfarne, 61, 71, 73, 85, 115
Livingstone, 11, 36, 39, 43, 155
Loyola, 37, 166
Lull, Raymund, 17, 36, 38, 39
Luther, Martin, 122, 127, 128, 166
Luxury, 178

Mackay, Alexander, 40, 182
Magyars, 16
Marquette, 41
Martin of Tours, 41
Martin, W. A. P., 181
Martyn, Henry, 38, 39
Mayhews, the, 170
Message, missionary, 55, 93, 95, 103, 184, 187, 192
Methodists, 140
Methods, missionary, 12, 30, 32, 51, 102
Mexico, 21
Migration, 15
Middle class, 162
Mills, Samuel J., 166
Monasticism, 41, 51, 57, 58, 87, 90, 96, 102, 104, 180

Money, 25, 32, 174
Mongolia, 47
Montevideo Congress, 27
Moravians, 11, 33, 36, 39, 41, 90, 122, 136, 138, 139, 153, 164, 166, 168, 169, 181
Morrison, Robert, 163
Moslems, 16, 17, 24, 27, 36, 41, 132, 154

Nationals, 18, 115
Nationalism, 14, 31, 127, 148, 167
Neesima, 39
Negroes, 11, 141
New England, 129
New England, Corporation for the Propagation of the Gospel in, 170
Newspapers, 165
Ninian, 65
Nitzschmann, 170
Non-Christian customs, 111

Opium Wars, 20
Organization, 34
Oswald, 10, 17, 61, 71, 107
Otto, 108
Outcastes, 33
Oxenbridge, 132

Palladius, 54, 55
Paraguay, 40
Patrick, 10, 12, 34, 35, 54, 55, 56, 85, 97, 103, 105, 106, 108, 114
Patteson, Bishop, 39
Paul, 35, 38, 43, 179
Paul the Apostle of the Congo, 36, 166
Paulinus, 72
Pegu, 47
Persecutions, 46
Persia, 21
Persistence of spiritual forces, 46
Pietism, 136, 166, 168, 169, 180
Pilgrims, 129
Pioneers, 40, 41
Plütschau, 137, 157
Policies, missionary, 11
Portugal, 21
Portuguese explorers, 151
Prayer, 104, 106, 117, 141, 174
Prideaux, 162
Principles, missionary, 38
Protestantism, 50

Qualities of missionaries, 39
Qualifications, missionary, 98

Race antagonism, 148
Ramabai, Pandita, 39
Reformation, Protestant, 49, 150
Rhenish Society, 138
Ricci, 41
Rice, Luther, 166
Roman Empire, 15, 16, 45
Rural work, 28
Russia, 16

Saravia, 41, 124, 133
Saxons, 60
Schmidt, George, 157
Schools, 164
Schwartz, 34, 36
Secularism, 31, 32, 148, 177, 182
Serampore, 11
Siam, 24, 47
Siamese, 24
Siberia, 47
Slessor, Mary, 40
Society for the Promotion of Christian Knowledge, 132, 170
Society for the Propagation of the Gospel in Foreign Parts, 170
South Africa, 24
South America, 11, 24, 27
Spanish explorers, 151
Spener, 136, 137
Spiritual lessons of history, 44
Spiritual life, 106
Student Volunteer Movement, 167, 175
Student Volunteers, 100
Success of Christian Missions, 175, 192
Support of missionaries, 101
Switzerland, 37, 63, 77
Sympathy, 43

Tamerlane, 47

Taylor, J. Hudson, 36
Theodore, 85
Thoburn, Isabella, 39
Tibet, 47
Tibetans, 173
Tiree, 67
Tongking, 47
Trade, 14, 20, 158, 171
Trading companies, 158
Tranquebar, 137, 157, 163, 170
Translation, 179, 181
Transportation, 163
Travel, 22, 33, 154
Truth, greatness of, 50
Turkey, 21
Turks, 47, 173

Uganda, 40, 156
Ultan, 81
Universities, 166
Universities Mission, 167

Verbeck, Guido, 39, 181
Volunteers, 96
Von Weltz, 41, 135, 169, 180

Wesley, John, 136, 140, 166
Wesley Revival, 168, 169, 170
West Indies, 141
Whitby, 72
Whitby, Synod of, 74, 75
Whitefield, George, 141
Whithorn, 57, 65
Whitman, Marcus, 41
Wilfrid, 34, 75
Williams College, 166
Williams, John, 41
Williams, Roger, 130

Xavier, Francis, 41, 49, 157

Ziegenbalg, 137, 157
Zinzendorf, 11, 34, 36, 138, 156, 166, 168, 170
Zwingli, 124, 128

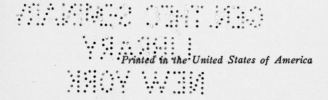